W9-AAJ-838

Fulfilling The Gospel Commission

A Video Series Featuring Mark Finley

Participant Study Guide

A Production of
Hart Research Center

Project Directors
Dan & Karen Houghton

Distributed by
Hart Publications
P.O. Box 8050
Riverside, CA 92515

Copyright © 1989, Hart Research Center

All rights reserved. No part of this publication may be
reproduced in any form without written permission from
Hart Research Center.

ISBN 1-878046-03-9 LITHO U.S.A. CP 42926

Endorsed for use throughout the
North American Division of the Seventh-day Adventist Church
by the NAD Materials and Marketing Committee.

Scripture quotations are taken from the
New International Version of the Bible,
unless indicated otherwise.

New International Version of the Bible
copyright 1973, 1978, 1984
International Bible Society

Table of Contents

Notes

Introduction

During my 20 years of involvement in evangelism and personal witnessing, I've become convinced that there are common soul-winning principles that can be applied in any given situation to transform human lives. I'm also convinced that, by studying these principles, you can make one of the most thrilling discoveries of your life.

We have three objectives for this seminar.

First, we'll talk about the <u>**spiritual preparation**</u> necessary for us to become a channel of God's blessing. Dwight L. Moody said, "The world is yet to see what God can do in and through and by and with the man that's totally consecrated to Him."

Secondly, we'll look at **motivation for witnessing**. What kind of powerful incentive can lead us to make soul-winning a priority in our life? And what are our ultimate objectives? Are we just trying to add people to the rolls of the church?

Finally, we'll talk about techniques: **how to witness more effectively,** how to be sensitive to others' needs, how to guide conversations from the secular to the spiritual, how to know when men and women are ready to receive Jesus Christ.

WHY WITNESS?

- Witnessing Brings Joy to God's Heart
- Witnessing is a Biblical Command
- Witnessing is the Heart's Response to Love
- Witnessing Contributes to Spiritual Life

Notes

Let's start by looking at a basic question: Why witness? Why make soul-winning a priority? We'll look at four important reasons, four great motives.

1. Witnessing brings joy to God's heart.

Witnessing has to do with the nature and personality of our God. He longs to reconcile every human being to Himself; it's not His will that a single person perish. All of heaven is interested in redeeming a lost race. That reflects the yearning heart of God.

Luke 15 presents us with three stories of things lost and found: a sheep, a coin, a boy. Each parable climaxes with someone rejoicing over having found the lost object or person. There is great rejoicing. And that, we are told, is how God feels about every sinner who comes to repentance. That's why witnessing brings joy to God's heart.

The Godhead from eternity past created on heaven's drawing board a strategy to save the lost. God the Son made the great sacrifice in this snake pit of a world. He made salvation possible with His own blood. The angels of heaven wing their way down to turn our steps toward the light. The Holy Spirit is poured out on the world to convict men and women of truth. Yes, God is eager to save the lost.

When I reach out, when I cooperate with Him, I become part of the great plan of salvation. What a thought! I can bring joy to the heart of my Creator.

There is much in our world to make God sad. God sees those starving babies throughout the world crying for milk. God sees the suffering patients in cancer wards. God sees the tragedy of broken families. God sees kids in back alleys shooting heroin. There is much to sadden the heart of God. But when we share Jesus Christ and become channels for God's transforming grace, when men and women are redeemed—God can rejoice greatly.

Why witness? First of all, because we have the privilege of bringing joy to the heart of our God.

2. Witnessing is a Biblical command.

You can sense the urgency of proclamation all through the New Testament. One example is Acts 13:47: "For this is what the Lord has commanded us: 'I have made you a light for the Gentiles, that you may bring salvation to the ends of the earth.'" What does God command us to do? Bring salvation to everyone, everywhere. A big part of being a Christian is being a light. When the church becomes ingrown and selfish, it fails its purpose in the world.

3. Witnessing is the heart's response to love.

When we come to Christ, receive His forgiveness and experience His love, there is born within us a desire to share that love. Love demands expression; love needs to be shared. And God's extraordinary love calls for whole-hearted expression.

Paul asks us to remember how patiently and perserveringly the Lord works for our salvation: "The Lord is not slow in keeping his promise, as some understand slowness. He is patient with you, not wanting anyone to perish, but everyone to come to repentance."(II Peter 3:9) God makes His unquenchable love apparent in His patient pursuit of needy individuals. Witnessing is our way of responding to such love.

Why witness? Because He first loved and forgave us.

> *"For this is what the Lord has commanded us: 'I have made you a light for the Gentiles, that you may bring salvation to the ends of the earth.' "*
> Acts 13:47

4. Witnessing contributes to spiritual life.

If you want a growing Christian experience, an alive Christian experience, find a way to share your faith. Witnessing stimulates our spiritual life like nothing else. It brings spiritual power:

"...strength to resist evil is best gained by aggressive service...."   *Acts of the Apostles, p. 105*

Are you struggling with pride or jealousy? Are you trying to overcome a lack of faith? Witnessing can help you be an overcomer.

Human beings have a natural tendency to shrink into a circle of selfishness. To grow we need to reach out. Mrs. White comments:

"...in order for us to develop a character like Christ's, we must share in His work."   *Desire of Ages, p. 142*

Sharing our faith will help us experience God's joy in ministering to others; we will begin to absorb His giving heart.

Many of us get stuck in a spiritual game of Annie Over, the ball goes up and almost over—and then comes right back. We are spiritually uplifted for a few weeks after a great sermon or retreat and then come right back down again to where we were before. We can change that up-and-back pattern by committing ourselves to witness as a way of life. By getting involved in sharing with others we receive power, we gain a depth to our Chrisitan experience, we become overcomers.

> *Witnessing stimulates our spiritual life like nothing else.*

What happens when . . . ?

Let's take a look at the book of Acts and what happened in 30 years through men and women consecrated to God; this will help us see and understand the dynamics involved in witnessing. This story actually begins with the training of the 12 disciples. Jesus took 12 quite ordinary men and poured His life into them. The disciples saw how He reached out to others day after day; they learned His lessons. And finally, Jesus gave them His Great Commission right before ascending to heaven: "Make disciples throughout the world." He promised He would be with them always as they shared the Gospel.

THE DISCIPLES' DIFFICULTIES

- Society was skeptical
- Society was influenced by Greek Philosophy
- Society was Secular and Materialistic
- Society Considered Christianity a Cult
- Society was Hungry for Real Spirituality

In the first chapter of Acts, we find 120 believers gathered in an upper room to seek God in prayer. For days they met together and prayed, believing in Christ's promise to empower them with His Spirit and make them His witnesses. Christ fulfilled His promise. He poured out His Spirit, the disciples began to share the Good News, and 3,000 were baptized.

A few chapters later, after more proclamation, 5,000 more were added to the movement. Now, this figure refers to "the number of men." One would guess that there were at least that many women and at least that many children who became believers along with the men. So, let's say we have 15,000 new members.

Notes

In a few short years, we've come from 12 to 120 to 3,000 to over 15,000. Something big is happening here. The book of Acts tells a grand story. The world was being turned upside down by Spirit-filled Christians.

But the story goes on. In Acts 9:31, we read that churches "were multiplied." Before, thousands were baptized, new believers multiplied. Now churches are multiplying—all over the Mediterranean world. In Acts 10, the Gospel has begun to invade other cultures. Cornelius and his household are converted. Now, the Good News is poised to spring out to men and women of every race, every creed, every culture. The book of Acts comes to a glorious climax with a report of tens of thousands of new converts. (Acts 21:20)

This movement started with a handful of believers in a secular society, in a culture that was anti-God and anti-Christian. It happened there and it's going to happen here. One day, a generation of Seventh-day Adventists will make that commitment: full surrender to Jesus Christ. One day a group of believers will say, "Lord, nothing else matters except sharing Your love with the world." And this earth is going to be flooded with the glory of God.

> *"Lord, nothing else matters except sharing Your love with the world."*

THINK IT OVER

1. What are the four primary motives for witnessing?

_____

_____

_____

_____

_____

_____

2. What single most important factor contributed to the rapid growth of the early church in Acts?

_____

_____

_____

_____

_____

_____

3. What obstacles do you personally face in becoming actively involved in witnessing?

_____

_____

_____

_____

_____

INTERACTION WITH THE WORD

(Please spend some time this week meditating on the following passages and responding to the questions.)

1. God expresses His heartbreaking eagerness to save the lost in Isaiah 65:1, 2. Try restating this passage in your own words.

   _____

   _____

   _____

   _____

2. How does James make very clear the part we can play in God's plan of redemption? (James 5:19)

   _____

   _____

   _____

   _____

3. Note how Paul makes witnessing an urgent command in II Timothy 4:1, 2.

   _____

   _____

   _____

   _____

4. How does Paul link sharing one's faith, or witnessing, with spiritual growth in Philemon 6?

   _____

   _____

   _____

   _____

My Child, I Need You

Thousands of lay people in the Adventist church today are discovering who they are in God's sight. They're sensing, with growing excitement, that they are called to be witnesses for Jesus Christ. They're sharing the Good News with friends, giving Bible studies, passing out literature, holding Daniel and Revelation seminars. They're taking advantage of the tools God has given us in this age.

> ### *There's a sense that it's no longer business as usual.*

Adventist lay people are realizing that we are living on the verge of the kingdom of God. There's a sense that it's no longer business as usual. Our brothers and sisters are giving their time, using their gifts, getting involved in service.

The church as a body.

Paul gives us a beautiful picture of what the church is all about in I Corinthians 12: "For we were all baptized by one Spirit into one body. . . Now the body is not made up of one part but of many." (v. 13, 14) Paul likens believers to members of Christ's body: "Now you are the body of Christ, and each one of you is a part of it." (v. 27) Just as each part of the human body has a special function which contributes to the whole, so each member of the church has a special ability, gift, or talent which makes it whole. And Paul emphasizes the fact that every member has a vital part to play. He writes, "The eye cannot say to the hand, 'I don't need you!' And the

head cannot say to the feet, 'I don't need you!' On the contrary, **those parts of the body that seem to be weaker are indispensable , . . ."** (v. 21, 22)

> ## One of Satan's greatest deceptions today is that soul-winning and evangelism are the work of the minister alone.

In this light we can't say, "I'm just a lay person; I don't have a degree from the seminary. I don't really have the knowledge or skill to do the work of witnessing." If we are believers in Christ, then we have a gift as part of His body. That's the promise of I Corinthians 12. Even if you feel your abilities are exceedingly modest, those gifts are really "indispensable." God has a role for you, a plan for you.

A young girl in Nigeria believed that God could use her, in spite of what appeared to be very small abilities. She couldn't read or write, but still wanted to tell her friends about Jesus. So, this girl memorized all the Sabbath School lesson memory verses for the quarter. Then she arranged them in a way that could lead people to an understanding of salvation.

The girl began visiting door-to-door every Sabbath afternoon. She'd greet her neighbors and tell them that she'd found a new faith; Jesus had become real to her. "Do you have a Bible?" she would ask. "I'd like to explain how I found Christ." Then she would ask the person to look up the verses, and she would explain their meaning. Soon the girl had won ten people to Christ.

Satan's deception.

Every one of us, as members of Christ's body, have received certain gifts for service. One of Satan's greatest deceptions in the Christian church today is that soul-winning and evangelism are the work of the minister alone. It's an old lie that has its roots in the Middle Ages when various heresies compromised the church. At that time, the clergy were elevated far above the laity, and their standing and role before God was sharply divided from that of their congregations.

Clergymen had special spiritual privileges as dispensers of the sacraments and interpreters of Scripture; the laity remained spiritually dependent. Clergymen had a special calling to do the work of God; the laity had only a secular vocation. And in heaven, clergymen would occupy special positions close to God which ordinary believers could not enjoy.

MISTAKEN DIVISION	
CLERGY	**LAITY**
Spiritually Strong	Spiritually Weak
Spiritual Calling	Secular Calling
Special Rewards	Ordinary Rewards

Revolutionary discovery!

But then came the Reformation. Students of Scripture made a startling discovery in I Peter 2:9: "But you are a chosen people, a royal priesthood, a holy nation, a people belonging to God,".. All believers are priests with direct access to God through Jesus Christ. Protestants armed with this truth were able to overturn the oppressive church dogma that had built up a bureaucracy between the individual and God.

But today many Protestants still unwittingly cling to parts of the old medievel thinking. **The attitude that I do my secular work, earn wages, and pay the preacher to witness for me, is part of that unscriptural division between clergy and laity.**

We need to rediscover the Reformation. Scripture declares that we are all a "royal priesthood." Whatever our individual gifts, we are all called to be ambassadors for Jesus Christ. Paul makes that clear in II Corinthians 5 where he talks about those who are in Christ becoming a new creation. The Apostle states: "All this is from God, who reconciled us to himself through Christ and gave us the ministry of reconciliation." (v. 18)

> ### *Whatever our individual gifts, we are all called to be ambassadors for Jesus Christ.*

Every human being reconciled to God is called to a "ministry of reconciliation." **We're all ministers!** Paul emphasizes the point in verse 20: "We are therefore Christ's ambassadors, as though God were making His appeal through us. We implore you on Christ's behalf: Be reconciled to God."

Our Lord wants to persuade men and women through us! We're His chosen instruments because we know something of what it's like to be reconciled to God. We're in a unique position to invite others to take advantage of the grace that has saved us.

William Carey, the London cobbler, saw himself in that light. A sign in his shop read: **"I cobble shoes to pay expenses, but soul-winning is my business."** He went on to become a great missionary in India. Whatever our job, whether we're a physician, construction worker, teacher, truck driver, or computer programmer, soul-winning is our business.

In I Corinthians 4:1, **all those who belong to Christ are declared to be "stewards (or ministers) of the mysteries of God."** (KJV) We've been entrusted with

marvelous truths to share. We each have different abilities and gifts, but we are all priests, all ambassadors, all stewards of divine truth.

Extraordinary church growth.

Everywhere in the Adventist world where this truth of the calling of ordinary believers has taken hold, the church is growing rapidly. The Philippines is a prime example. The church there has grown by 200,000 members in 28 years. **And 60 percent of those baptisms came as a result of lay efforts.** In places like East Africa and Mexico, where a pastor has 20 or 30 churches, he must entrust much of his work to lay people. The result? Tremendous growth. The chart below shows that where the ratio of pastor to member is very low, the church tends to grow most rapidly.

This, of course, doesn't mean that we need to reduce the number of pastors in the field. It indicates simply that the more lay members have to be involved in the work of the church, the more the church grows. These people become priests, ambassadors, stewards of God's mysteries.

Notes

CHURCH GROWTH RATIO

TERRITORY	PASTOR-MEMBER RATIO	GROWTH RATE
Europe	1 to 169	1.25%
Japan	1 to 100	1.50%
North America	1 to 172	1.70%
South America	1 to 628	8.92%
Inter-America	1 to 830	6.91%
East Africa	1 to 1,000	12.00%
Mexican Union	1 to 1,000	12.00%
South Philippine Union	1 to 1,000	12.00%

Figures are derived from the Statistical Report of the Seventh-day Adventist Church issued on June 30, 1988. In a few instances estimates are made from existing data.

> *Lay men and women are the key to Fulfilling the Great Commission.*

And that is what we are all called to become. Lay men and women are the key to Fulfilling the Great Commission. That's the only way the Good News is going to cover the globe. So, please never say, "I'm just a layman." Andrew was just a layman, but he led Peter to Christ. And Peter the layman, the fisherman, won 3,000 to Christ in one day. The book of Acts blazes with the glory of lay preaching. Farmers and merchants and sheep herders turned the world upside down as ambassadors of Jesus Christ.

Dwight L. Moody was a layman, won to Christ by another layman, and he rocked two continents with the power of the gospel. William Miller the farmer, Joseph Bates the sea captain, and James White the teacher created the Advent movement that awakened a slumbering church to the reality of Christ's coming.

God is gathering lay people around the world for a final movement at the climax of earth's history. He will pour out His Spirit on them as they use their gifts to proclaim the Good News. I pray that we will all be part of that glorious army.

> *"But you are a chosen people, a royal priesthood, a holy nation, a people belonging to God."*
> **I Peter 2:9**

DISCUSSION AND SHARING TIME

(This is best done if participants break up into small groups.)

1. What did the Reformers discover about the role of the laity in the church?

_____

_____

_____

_____

_____

2. What "ministry" do each of us have?

_____

_____

_____

_____

_____

3. How have your ideas about your role as a church member changed over the years?

_____

_____

_____

_____

_____

4. Why did you join this training program?

_____

_____

_____

_____

_____

INTERACTION WITH THE WORD

1. In Ephesians 6 Paul describes the armor that enables a believer to successfully "stand against the devil's schemes." Which part of that armor seems to relate to our agility, our moving forward in the Christian life? (v. 15)

_____

_____

_____

_____

_____

2. John opens his first epistle with a statement about what he has seen and heard and touched. (v. 1-4) He explains why he can testify about eternal life. What does he say is his motivation in communicating this Good News?

_____

_____

_____

_____

_____

3. In Revelation 12 we get a condensed view of the history of Christ and His church, their great struggle against Satan, the Dragon, and their final triumph. Verse 11 reveals the resources God's people use in overcoming the evil one. What are they?

_____

_____

_____

_____

_____

4. Luke 5:1-11 recalls the incident which gave Simon Peter
an unforgettable picture of what it means to be a fisher of
men. Peter caught the vision. Jesus had met him in his
own work-a-day world of fishing boats, sail cloth, nets, and
piles of glistening fish. And Jesus showed Himself master
of that world, capable of performing miracles in it. On
that basis He issued His historic call: "From now on you
will catch men."

Try to imagine Jesus coming into your work environment
right now, whatever it might be. Think of how He could
demonstrate His Lordship over your occupation. What
words would He use to make His call as real for you as it
was for those fishermen?

_____

_____

_____

_____

_____

_____

_____

_____

_____

_____

_____

_____

Notes

Lord, Open My Eyes

People who change the world invariably have a vision, something that propels them into action. In this chapter we'll discuss two great principles of soul-winning that can propel you into action. If these principles are firmly in your mind, you will be successful in sharing your faith. Without them, you will fail in the long run.

The first principle is this: Churches grow as they profoundly believe it is God's will for them to grow.

Church Growth Conscience.

It is vital to develop a conviction about our purpose in life. Some people call it a "burden for souls." Pulsating within the heart and mind of every soul-winner is a desire to win men and women for Jesus Christ. It's not just a belief one gives assent to. It must become a burning conviction, a matter of conscience.

Conscience is that still, small voice which prompts us to do right. It's a voice that we can't easily ignore. **A Church Growth Conscience prompts us to share Christ with the people around us.** That's a big part of our purpose in life. The church exists in order to grow.

CHURCH GROWTH CONSCIENCE

The conviction that it's God's will for the church to grow

So, how do we get this mindset that prompts us to reach out? We can't just pound the idea into our heads; we need something more inspiring. The story of John Henry Dunent gives us an important clue.

Dunent, a brilliant banker and economist, was sent by a Swiss banking company in 1859 to the Alps where Napoleon III was fighting the Austrian army. He needed to get Napoleon's permission for a financial venture in Algeria. Shortly after arriving on the scene, Dunent watched as the French and Austrian armies lined up to do battle. The cannons roared, musket volleys rang out, lines of infantry charged and counterattacked.

Young Dunent watched all this horror-stricken. He'd never imagined there could be such carnage; men lay all over the battlefield. That evening 15,000 dead or dying human beings sprawled on the ground as far as the eye could see.

This heart-wrenching scene propelled Dunent into action. He could no longer remain merely a spectator. All night he labored along with other volunteers, dragging the wounded to makeshift hospitals, bandaging wounds as best he could.

After that experience he just couldn't go back to banking. Money no longer seemed that important. A larger vision filled his mind. John Henry Dunent began traveling around Europe, visiting all the heads of state who would listen, and pleading eloquently for the cause of world peace. He established what has become known today as the International Red Cross. Eventually, Dunent won the Nobel Peace Prize.

> *The best way to get a Church Growth Conscience is to take a close, prayerful look at the cross.*

See Christ on the field of battle, wrestling alone in the vast terror of the world's sin. He was willing to walk into hell with His eyes wide open, willing to be forsaken by the Father, in order to rescue human beings from their fate. If we really get a glimpse of Christ's heroic suffering up close, we won't be able to remain spectators. We'll be compelled to plead for others to accept the peace which God so graciously offers.

So, meditate on the cross and pray for a Church Growth Conscience. Make it a regular petition: **"Lord please give me a burden for the lost human beings all around me. Give me an inspired desire to see men and women reconciled to You."**

John Knox fervently prayed, "Lord, give me Scotland! Or I die." General Booth, founder of the Salvation Army, once wrote in the royal guestbook, "Some men's ambition is fame...some men's ambition is wealth. But your majesty, my ambition is the souls of men and women."

Soul-winners have a conviction in their hearts; they also have a special vision, eyes to see. This is the second great principle of soul-winning:

CHURCH GROWTH EYES

The ability to see people
as Jesus saw them

Church Growth Eyes.

To have Church Growth Eyes we need the perspective of our Savior. When Jesus looked at people, He didn't just see them as they were; He saw what they could become. When Nicodemus came calling at night, Jesus saw more than a leader of the religious opposition; He saw a man secretly longing for spiritual truth. Jesus didn't just see in Peter a loud-mouthed fisherman; by faith He glimpsed a

mighty preacher, humbled and empowered by the Spirit. When Christ looked over at the thief crucified beside Him, He saw much more than a man punished for his crimes, He caught a glimmer of desperate hope and turned it into faith.

Everywhere Jesus went He saw spiritual possibilities; He saw potential candidates for the kingdom in the most unlikely circumstances. We need to see with His eyes. What do we see in that person sitting next to us at the office? What do we see in the mechanic who tunes up our car? What do we see in the neighbor across the street?

We can't be so wrapped up in ourselves and our schedules that we fail to see candidates for the kingdom. We need Church Growth Eyes, the sensitivity of Christ.

Our Circle of Influence.

And that circle starts with our **family;** that's where most of us have the greatest influence. Is there someone in your family who has not found a saving knowledge of Jesus Christ or someone who is drifting away from his or her religious roots? Begin to see them as candidates for the kingdom.

Often our family members may appear the hardest to reach. "Oh, they're not interested; they'll never listen," we say. But never underestimate the power of God, and never underestimate the influence of a loving witness. Even those who seem most indifferent have moments when they become susceptible to spiritual influences.

Next, think about your **close friends**; people you feel comfortable talking to. Have you spoken with them about your faith, about what really matters most in your life? Begin to see candidates for the kingdom among those you interact with socially.

What about your **work associates**? You're involved with people every day on the job. How can you see with the eyes of Christ in that environment? Look for candidates.

Notes

Finally, think of your more **casual acquaintances**, people who may not be friends, but whom you see now and then. God often puts us in the right place at the right time in order to reach someone.

Now that you've begun to picture your Circle of Influence, write down names in each sphere. Get specific. This will sharpen both your conviction and your Church Growth Eyes.

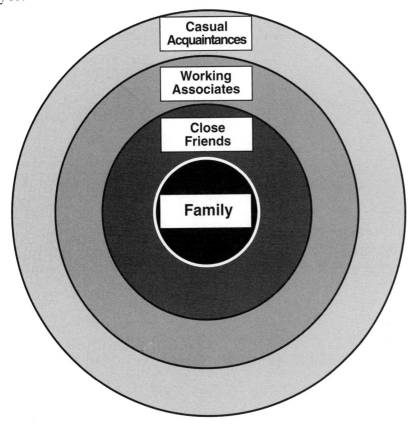

Family
_____
_____
_____
_____

Close Friends
_____
_____
_____
_____

Working Associates
_____
_____
_____
_____

Casual Aquaintances
_____
_____
_____
_____

My wife once asked me to go to a certain barber in our town because he'd expressed an interest in spiritual things while cutting our son's hair. Fortunately, my wife had Church Growth Eyes and saw in this man a potential candidate for God's kingdom.

> *Never underestimate*
> *the power of God,*
> *and never underestimate*
> *the influence*
> *of a loving witness.*

I went to this barber a few times and got to know him. Then, during my second or third visit, I began reading a newspaper while he cut my hair and threw out a little bait. I said, "You know, the more I read the news, the worse things seem to get."

He replied, "I get that impression too; things are getting pretty bad, aren't they?"

"You read about plane crashes and hijackings, about war and famine," I went on. "The more I read this stuff, the more troubled I get."

Then the barber remarked, "You think the news is scary? Wait until you read the book of Revelation." I asked what he meant and he described fire coming down from heaven and beasts rising from the sea and said it was enough to give him nightmares.

"You know what, though," I told him, "Revelation really has a hopeful message." And I told this man about the hope this book presents of the coming of Christ and the creation of a new world. "It's not really so scary if you look at it that way," I said.

> ## *All around us are men and women opening up to the Gospel.*

The barber responded enthusiastically: "Do you think we might get together so that you could explain more of Revelation to me?"

This casual conversation led to systematic Bible studies. Within a few months, I had the privilege of baptizing this man. God simply used a casual acquaintance, a spark of interest in spiritual things, and a willingness to see a potential candidate for the kingdom.

All around us every day are men and women who are opening up to the Gospel, people who are reaching some point of receptivity. We need to see those people with Church Growth Eyes; we need to be motivated by a Church Growth Conscience and seek to win them. I hope our prayer will be: "Lord, please open my eyes; help me be sensitive to the people around me so I can reach out as Your hand to a world of lost men and women."

> ## *"The Lord is not slow in keeping His promise . . . He is patient with you, not wanting anyone to perish, but everyone to come to repentance."*
> II Peter 3:9

Notes

DISCUSSION AND SHARING TIME

(This is best done if participants break up into small groups.)

1. What does the expression "Church Growth Eyes" mean to you personally?

_____

_____

_____

_____

2. Can you think of a few unlikely candidates for the kingdom whom Jesus looked at with Church Growth Eyes?

_____

_____

_____

_____

3. Who among your circle of acquaintances are the most likely candidates for the kingdom of God right now? Why?

_____

_____

_____

_____

4. How would you detect if an individual is interested in spiritual things?

_____

_____

_____

_____

INTERACTION WITH THE WORD

1. Acts 20:19-24 gives us a glimpse of a man with a Church Growth Conscience. Write down the phrases that speak to you best of what it means to have a burden for souls.

_____

_____

_____

_____

_____

2. In John 4, how did Jesus attempt to get His disciples to see with Church Growth Eyes in a place where their prejudices got in the way?

_____

_____

_____

_____

_____

3. Note how Paul expresses his passionate concern for the spiritual welfare of others in I Thessalonians 3:6-8.

_____

_____

_____

_____

_____

4. Put in your own words Paul's great affirmation in Romans 1:14-16 about sharing the Gospel.

_____

_____

_____

_____

_____

Notes

ASSIGNMENT

Begin praying for relatives, friends, work associates or acquaintances who are unchurched or don't know Christ. You may have several people in mind after the discussion. Ask God to show you how you can reach them. Ask Him to give you a Church Growth Conscience.

The Master's Methods

A renowned surgeon named Lewis Evans once traveled to Korea to visit a colleague who was working as a missionary there. Dr. Evans accompanied his friend to a remote village where a sick woman required major surgery. He watched as this physician calmly and steadily performed the seven-hour operation in stifling heat and under primitive conditions.

Later, as the two men chatted, Dr. Evans rather playfully asked, "Hey Doc, how much do you get for an operation like that out here? In the States it would be worth at least $15,000."

The other man answered by pulling out a dented copper coin from his drawer. He explained that was all the patient had to give. But then he said, "First, I get this dented copper coin, but second, I have the priceless awareness that Christ is working for seven hours through these fingers to touch and heal one of His children." That is Christianity!

It is our privilege to touch other people in the same way that Christ did. That, in fact, is His model for evangelism. The book of John gives us several vignettes which picture just how Jesus set about to change the world.

> *"I have the awareness that Christ is working for seven hours through these fingers. . . ."*

How Jesus Related to People.

The story begins in the very first chapter of John, verses 37 and 38. Here we see two disciples of John the Baptist, who've heard Christ speak, begin to follow Him away from the crowd. Jesus turned to them and asked, "What do you want?" I think that little question is quite revealing. The Master didn't start with His agenda, but with theirs. He didn't approach those two men with His pre-arranged program; He began where they were and gradually led them to Himself.

> *The Master didn't start with His agenda, but with theirs. He began where they were and gradually led them to Himself.*

We see this more clearly in the incidents that follow. John 2 records Christ's visit to a **wedding feast at Cana**. During the celebration, the host ran out of wine. This was a social disaster; to run out of refreshment for all those guests present was humiliating. Jesus' mother learned of the host's anxiety and told her Son about it. He proceeded to turn water in six stone jars into choice wine, the best of the feast. Problem solved.

This miracle shows Christ's willingness to care for people's needs, period—even ones that seem unspiritual. He saved the host from humiliation—quietly, tactfully. Jesus met the need of the present moment.

In John 3 we find Christ talking with a Pharisee who had asked for a meeting in the dead of night. **Nicodemus** had become aware that he needed more than a formal

religion; he was looking for something more than ritual and tradition. So, Jesus showed him exactly what he was looking for, and how to get it: "You must be born again!" This religious leader was open that evening to spiritual direction, so Jesus met him on that level.

Then we come to the fourth chapter of John. Christ was passing through Samaria and encountered the woman at the well. He met her need very skillfully by giving her a measure of respect. Stepping around centuries of prejudice and animosity he asked, "Will you give Me a drink?"

This woman had gone through six husbands; the men in her village regarded her as a mere plaything. She had come alone to this well; the other village women avoided her. So, Jesus offered this outcast emotional support, treating her with kindness, and offering her something wonderful: water that ensures we'll never thirst again. He very carefully led her from where she was, focused on getting water from a deep well, to an understanding of Himself as the Giver of eternal life.

John 5 shows us a very dramatic healing by the Pool of Bethesda. Again Jesus was meeting a human being precisely at the point of his present need. This poor paralytic, who'd been lying in despair for 38 years, wanted to move, to walk! So Jesus asked, "Do you want to get well?" and awakened a spark of faith in the paralytic. Responding to Jesus' command, he rose to his feet, his wasted body suddenly made whole again. Jesus met his physical need.

> ***Christ met whatever need people had, whether physical, emotional, social or spiritual.***

This is how Jesus worked. He didn't tell the humiliated host at Cana he had to be born again. That wasn't something he could handle then. He met the need he was feeling at the moment. He didn't tell the paralytic about living water; that would not have registered. He helped him get up and walk.

In John 6, we find Christ confronted with thousands of hungry people on a hillside overlooking the Lake of Galilee. They had a definite need, as the whimpering of the children made plain. The disciples suggested that the crowds be sent away to find nourishment in the neighboring villages. But Jesus insisted that they as evangelists must meet the need with their meager provisions. The Master prayed, the bread and fish were broken, and thousands ate their fill. Problem solved. Need met.

Here's a summary of what Jesus did in the first six chapters of John:

JESUS' METHOD

Discover a Felt Need and Meet It!

EVENT	FELT NEED
Wedding Feast	Social Embarrassment
Nicodemus	Genuine Spirituality
Woman at Well	Emotional Support
Man at Pool	Physical Healing
Hungry Multitude	Physical Nourishment

Jesus is the One who can meet every human need. **His method of evangelism is simply this: to reach people where they are, touch them at the point of their need, and give them a glimpse of His magnificent love.**

Jesus' method of evangelism will revolutionize our church. The Lord's strategy is nicely summarized in the book *Ministry of Healing*, page 143:

> "Christ's method alone will give true success in reaching the people. The Savior mingled with men as one who desired their good. He showed His sympathy for them, ministered to their needs, and won their confidence. Then He bade them, 'Follow Me.'"

Jesus first ministered to people's needs. Then He issued the challenge: "Follow Me." Our Lord's method of evangelism goes beyond memorized speeches and canned presentations; it's as rich and dynamic as life itself. Every day we rub shoulders with people who have all kinds of needs: physical, emotional, mental, and spiritual. Christ is eager to meet those needs through us as we show concern for people's loneliness, sorrow, and heartache, as we show an interest in an individual's hopes and dreams.

---

*Christ's method alone
will bring
true success
in reaching people.*

Felt Needs and Ultimate Needs.

Here it's useful to make a distinction between a felt need and an ultimate need. **A felt need is an area of life where an individual already senses that he's in need of help.** It's a perceived need. Many harried businessmen, for example, have a felt need of alleviating stress. A cigarette smoker's felt need is help in kicking his habit.

An ultimate need, however, is what human beings need most—in the long run. We believe that every person on this planet needs God most in their lives. Reconciliation with Him is man's ultimate need.

Many of our contemporaries do not sense such a need yet. They are only interested in having their felt needs met. However, the good news is that these felt needs can become avenues through which a person becomes aware of his or her ultimate need. Meeting felt needs breaks down barriers and helps people open up to the spiritual dimension of life.

Dave was one who showed no interest in the Bible or religion. His wife had become a Christian through her interest in Bible prophecy. But Dave had grown bitter about God after the death of their three-year-old son. Still, he did have a definite felt need. Working hard as a salesman in Chicago usually left him quite knotted-up at the end of the day. When his wife told him about some stress-reduction seminars we were conducting in the area, he was interested.

> *Meeting felt needs breaks down barriers and helps people open up to the spiritual dimension of life.*

During the seminar we talked about the physical dimensions of stress and also the emotional dimensions—how to resolve resentment and anger. Dave was on the edge of his seat. When we came to the spiritual dimensions of the problem, he wasn't quite as receptive, but still he read the seminar materials.

We followed up that seminar with an evangelistic series. Although his wife attended, Dave wouldn't come.

But he began listening to the tapes from the series which she brought home. Then one day he called me up and said, "I want to be baptized. How long do you have to study the Bible with me?" I went over right away, of course, and found that he had studied and accepted all the basic teachings of Scripture and the Adventist faith. **The turning point in his life came when he sensed that Adventists were caring enough to minister to his physical needs and help him alleviate stress.**

There are many people who may not show any apparent interest in things of the Spirit, but who will open up wonderfully when someone meets them where they are, in the area of a felt need.

Ellen White says it clearly:

"Many have no faith in God and have lost confidence in man. But they appreciate acts of sympathy and helpfulness. As they see one with no inducement of earthly praise or compensation coming to their homes, ministering to the sick, feeding the hungry, clothing the naked, comforting the sad, and tenderly pointing all to Him. . . as they see this, their hearts are touched. Gratitude springs up, faith is kindled. They see that God cares for them, and as His Word is opened they are prepared to listen."   *Medical Ministry, p. 247*

We need to meet people where they are. This is the divine strategy: men and women who sense they are ambassadors for Christ reaching out with His love to meet physical, mental, and emotional needs. But through all this, we have one great objective. Christ was interested not just in turning water into wine, but in revealing the wine of the Gospel to His contemporaries. He was interested in more than just providing the multitudes with a good meal; He longed to show them the Bread of Life. **Everything we do as believers has one ultimate purpose: to lead people to Jesus Christ.**

Now some may object to this. It may sound manipulative—we help people only because we want them baptized. Shouldn't we just meet people's felt needs and leave the rest up to God?

Well, it's true that we should be very willing to help people no matter what their ultimate decision may be about Christ or the church. But we must never forget what a human being's ultimate need is: to be reconciled to God. That is the most legitimate need we have as human beings. As believers we have a responsibility to try to meet that need. Helping a person make a spiritual decision is not any less "caring" than helping them quit smoking.

What really makes the difference between efforts that are manipulative and efforts that aren't is simply whether we are acting in love or not. Jesus' compassion is the key. Love in feeding people, love in healing people, love in evangelizing people. That's what fulfills the law of Christ.

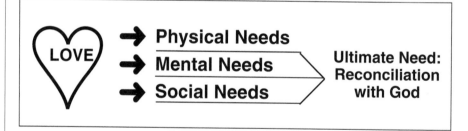

Once my father took me on a tour of the Bowery in New York City to show me the environment in which he'd been raised as a child. While stopped at a red light, we looked over and saw four drunks lying on the sidewalk. One drunk dragged himself to his feet and began lumbering over to the car; I could smell him coming. His shirt and trousers were filthy and torn. There were scars on his unshaven face. He leaned over and said, "Can't you spare a man a dollar?"

I didn't want to give him money he'd use on more alcohol so we began rummaging around for something to give him to eat. I handed him an apple. He smiled and

showed his toothless gums. "I can't eat that apple!" he said. So I peeled a banana and gave it to him.

There are some moments in your life that are imprinted on your brain cells forever. This drunk reached through the window, took my head in his hands, pulled my face to his, and said, "Thank you, Jesus." Then he turned and walked across the street.

We, together, are the hands of Christ, the words of Christ, to the world. Our feet are to be Jesus' feet. As the apostle Paul powerfully proclaimed, "Now then, we are ambassadors for Christ."(II Corinthians 5:20) His great method of evangelism is to be our method. May we all commit ourselves to reaching out in love just as He did.

> *God has no eyes in this world except our eyes, no mouth in this world except our mouth.*

DISCUSSION AND SHARING TIME

(Interaction in small groups is especially important as people begin sharing about their experiences in witnessing).

1. Give another example of Jesus' method of evangelism.

_____

_____

_____

_____

_____

_____

2. What are the felt needs in people around you that you are most aware of?

_____

_____

_____

_____

_____

3. Have you seen people open up to spiritual things after believers have met some of their other needs? Share some experiences.

_____

_____

_____

_____

_____

4. Talk about last week's assignment. Did you begin to pray for someone specifically? Share about these people and their needs and possible ways of reaching them.

_____

_____

_____

_____

_____

ASSIGNMENT

Try to meet a felt need in the person or persons you've begun praying for. Get to know them a little better; try to see where they are feeling a need. Just listening may be something valuable. But, as far as possible, see how God can use you to meet a need.

INTERACTION WITH THE WORD

1. How did Jesus emphasize the importance of meeting seemingly "unspiritual" needs? (Matthew 10:42)

_____

_____

_____

_____

2. Romans 12:9-15 is a wonderful passage related to ministering to others. List ways in which these verses suggest we can help people.

_____

_____

_____

_____

3. What striking image does Paul give us that embodies the idea of nurturing people into the faith? (I Thessalonians 2:7, 8)

_____

_____

_____

_____

4. Study Jesus' encounter with the woman at the well in John 4. Note the different needs which Jesus met or identified during His short dialogue with this woman.

_____

_____

_____

_____

_____

Notes

Reaching the Unreached

I once saw a cartoon which fascinated me. It pictured two emaciated men chained to the walls inside a prison cell. Just outside the cell bars, two guards stood with machine guns pointed at the prisoners. Out in the courtyard two large tanks aimed their huge guns at the tiny cell and its two frail men. Beyond the courtyard stood a high, thick wall with embedded glass and barbed wire along the top. In large towers on the wall other guards pointed their machine guns at the cell. And, surrounding it all, was a wide moat filled with snakes and alligators.

But in that little cell, one prisoner was telling the other, "Don't worry, brother, I've got a plan."

Jesus looked down on a world hopelessly shackled in sin, tragically imprisoned by the evil one, and He said, "Don't worry, brother, I have a plan." And what a plan it was! Our world was enshrouded in darkness regarding who God really was. Satan had pictured Him as an exacting, condemning diety, responsible for all the suffering on the planet. How could God reveal His true nature? By giving us an unforgettable, flesh-and-blood picture. Christ has demonstrated God's character and proven His unconditional love on Satan's ground. God became flesh not just to lecture us about the nature of His love, but to show it among real men and women with real problems and needs.

We get a remarkable summary of the mission of Christ in Luke 19:41. The Savior was riding in triumphal procession toward Jerusalem; His life on earth was approaching its terrible and glorious climax on the cross. Luke records: "And when he was come near, he beheld the city, and wept over it." (KJV)

That wonderful phrase "when he was come near" pictures the mission of Christ. We serve a God who is not far off but who has come very near. Christ comes near human beings, touching the eyes of the blind, the limbs of the lame, the rotting flesh of lepers, and making all whole again. He touches the cold form of a little girl and imparts life. Jesus walks through the dusty roads of Judea, crosses meadows where sheep graze, rides across Lake Galilee on fishing boats. He is altogether here—here to minister to broken bodies and broken hearts.

> ## *Jesus did not merely tell, He showed.*

Matthew has his own short summary of the ministry of this God-in-the-flesh: "Jesus went through all the towns and villages, teaching in their synagogues, preaching the good news of the kingdom and healing every disease and sickness." (Matthew 9:35)

Notice that Jesus characteristically combined preaching, teaching, and healing. He did not merely tell, He showed. He began with the physical, mental, and social concerns which occupied the thoughts of most of His contemporaries. He led people step-by-step to ever clearer conceptions of what His kingdom was all about. His every act of mercy became a symbol of divine mercy interrupting human sin. His every act of healing became a metaphor for salvation.

Jesus' three-and-a-half-year ministry was a bridge laid down between heaven and earth. It extended the whole way, stretching from the most rebellious inhabitant of the planet to the very throne room of God Almighty. Every human being could find a place on that bridge that would take him or her from precisely where they were all the way to reconciliation with God.

We are called to extend Christ's ministry on earth; we are to become a bridge today. As a body of believers we can meet people at whatever point of interest or disinterest they may be and, by meeting their needs, lead them along the bridge toward God. Whenever the church is reaching out in love to meet physical, mental, and social concerns, it is forming a bridge to spiritual concerns.

It's useful to try to look at the bridge we can form to reach all kinds of people in some detail:

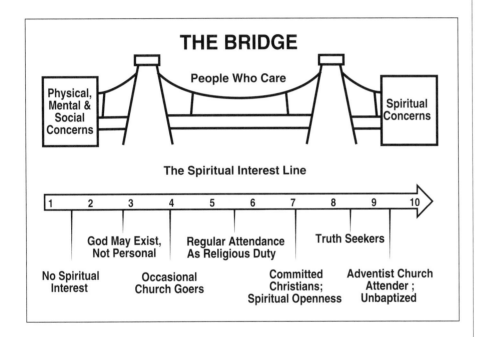

We can break the bridge up into different levels of spiritual interest, from one to ten. One represents the lowest degree of interest, ten the highest. Here we represent the whole spectrum of humanity, from the committed atheist to the nominal Christian to the believer earnestly seeking truth.

Try to think of some characters in the Bible from this perspective. The Roman centurion presiding over the crucifixion, for example, would probably be a one or two. He'd been trained to honor militaristic gods and probably just wanted to get the execution over with so he could go out for some wine with the boys. But still, the way Jesus died had a profound impact on this man.

What about Nicodemus? He came seeking Jesus, even if a bit uncertainly. This Pharisee felt a longing for spiritual meaning in his life. He would fall around number seven, the point of spiritual openness.

We can divide this bridge or interest line into two main parts. Numbers one to six represent people who are not overtly spiritual; they're not consciously seeking God. Numbers seven through ten represent those who are open to or actively seeking spiritual truth.

Now, ask yourself where most people in society fall. Looking at the world today, looking at what most people pursue most of the time, we'd have to conclude that they're below point seven. They have not yet developed a conscious openness to religious truth.

That's why it's so important to have a variety of outreach activities which meet the majority of people where they are. We need to lead them along that bridge, step by step. And that's why an invitation to study the Bible may not attract that many; its appeal is limited to those individuals who've progressed to point seven and beyond.

Still, there are many of our neighbors whom God has moved to the point of openness, people like Cornelius and the Ethiopian eunuch, who are waiting for someone to meet their spiritual longing. And so direct invitations to a Revelation Seminar or Bible study or evangelistic meeting form a vital part of our bridge.

Never discount the possibility that the Holy Spirit may have nurtured a real desire for spiritual truth in that neighbor who gives no evidence of any religious inclination.

What matters is that we keep reaching out to people at whatever point they are on this line of spiritual interest. All it takes is getting to know someone; we'll soon be able to get an idea of what they're receptive to.

> *What matters is that
> we keep reaching out
> to people. . . .*

Avoiding two witnessing mistakes.

Once we grasp this idea of a spiritual interest line we are freed from two witnessing hang-ups. **The first is the sense that we must twist a decision for Christ out of everyone we have an opportunity to speak with.** If a person says yes to Jesus right then and there, we succeed; if the person says no, we fail. I remember going door-to-door and inviting people to study the Bible. If the person wasn't interested, I'd walk away feeling guilty, and thinking, "If only I'd said the right word I could have been a better witness." We don't need this kind of guilt trip.

Now I simply try to move people along the line of spiritual interest. If I find someone who's at point seven or beyond, wonderful; I can take them directly to spiritual concerns. But, if I find someone who's, say, at point four, an occasional church-goer who just tries to be good enough to get by, then I don't try to push him to a commitment right away—and perhaps drive him back to point two. I simply try to encourage him to be a five. I might say something about how much my church fellowship has meant to me or I might talk about how a relationship with Christ makes "being good" much more of a pleasure.

Our task as part of Christ's great bridge between heaven and earth is simply to help move people from their present concerns to more and more ultimate concerns. We provide the nudges that open people up a little more. We demonstrate the love that awakens them to God's love a little more.

Now we come to **the second witnessing hang-up: That is the assumption that people must always progress along the spiritual interest line by the numbers, the assumption that they can only be moved to the next point.** Just as we can be too pushy in our outreach, we can also be over-cautious. We need to accept the fact that sometimes a two can become a seven overnight. The Holy Spirit can propel people quite a long ways in a short time.

A Chicago yuppie had it made—a well-paying job, an exclusive condominium in the city, and a cabin in Colorado where he and his wife could go for skiing every other weekend. He seemed totally insulated from any need of God. But one day he came home from work and found a note from his wife: "Dear, I'm gone and I'm not coming back. I met somebody else." The bottom of his life dropped out. A little later he saw a handbill in the mail which advertised, "How to find peace of mind and how to put your life together." Mark found himself in the front row of one of my meetings. Suddenly he was very needy, and very open.

> ## *We need to be ready when a person suddenly feels compelled to find God.*

So we need to be ready for those moments of illumination, those times of intense openness, when a person who has hardly given God a thought until today, suddenly feels compelled to find Him. We need to move with the Holy

Physical Needs

• Breathe Free
• Cooking
• Fitness

Emotional Needs

• Grief Recovery
• Divorce Recovery
• Stress

The Body of Christ Gifted for Service

Spiritual Needs

• Bible Studies
• Literature Ministry
• Daniel
• Revelation
• Evangelistic Outreach

• Music
• Fellowship Dinners
• Parenting
• Youth Activities

Social Needs

Spirit's movements in a person's life. If they are slow and regular, then we accompany that progression patiently. If they are sudden and intense, we reinforce that moment of illumination and show how it can become a serious commitment to Christ.

The church as a whole is best equipped to do this, to be the kind of bridge that meets people wherever they are, able to meet whatever needs a person might present. The chart above pictures the way your congregation can function as the body of Christ gifted for service.

The church is to be an active, dynamic agency filled with men and women of varying gifts, varying talents— people who day-by-day come in contact with different individuals.

We are gifted for service.

We meet emotional needs through grief recovery seminars.

We meet physical needs through cooking classes and stress seminars.

We meet social needs through hospitality groups and simple person-to-person interaction.

We meet spiritual needs by studying the Bible with people, taking them to meetings, and sharing our testimony.

God wants His church to be involved in every sector of society.

We need Christian secretaries, Christian mechanics, Christian professors—men and women who win others for Jesus Christ wherever they are. The church is to be the place where all of us get strength for our service during the week. Wouldn't it be wonderful to be part of a fellowship like that, a church where each member sensed that they are a minister, a church which is alive and growing? That is the church of the future.

We have a marvelous calling. It's not to be part of something small and sporadic. The church is not a fire-cracker that sputters out; it's a worldwide explosion waiting to happen. The church is not some little drip of water in the world; it's building up to a tremendous outpouring—the latter rain. We can all be part of a great prophetic movement of destiny sweeping toward the climax of history.

We can be part of those who illuminate the whole world with the light of the Gospel of Jesus Christ.

> *"Arise, shine, for your Light has come, and the glory of the Lord rises upon you."*
>
> Isaiah 60:1

DISCUSSION AND SHARING TIME

1. Think of a few characters from the Bible and try to place them on the line of spiritual interest. Where would they fit? The Ethiopian eunuch? Nebuchadnezzar? Ruth? The thief on the cross? Pilate?

_____

_____

_____

_____

2. Where are the majority of people in your community on the spiritual interest line?

_____

_____

_____

_____

3. How did you progress in your own spiritual journey? Was it a gradual progression or more of a sudden revelation?

_____

_____

_____

_____

4. Talk about last week's assignment. How did it go? Were you able to identify or meet felt needs in those you are praying for? Share results. Talk about problems.

_____

_____

_____

_____

_____

Notes

ASSIGNMENT

Engage the person you want to reach in conversation this week. Try to identify about where they are on the spiritual interest line. Gently encourage them to share their beliefs, their approach to life. See if, by sharing something from your own experience and by encouraging them, you can begin moving them to the next point of spiritual interest.

INTERACTION WITH THE WORD

1. Paul provides a great example of meeting people where they are and identifying with their needs and concerns. Note the very different groups he was able to relate to in I Corinthians 9:19-23.

   _____
   _____
   _____
   _____
   _____
   _____

2. What excellent advice does Paul give in Colossians 4:5, 6 that could serve as a motto for those seeking to make friendly conversation a means of sharing their faith?

   _____
   _____
   _____
   _____
   _____
   _____

3. Study carefully how Paul explained his beliefs to a group of Epicurean and Stoic philosophers. Trace how he tried to take them from where they were as polytheists to a few points up on the scale of spiritual interest. (Acts 17:22-31)

_____

_____

_____

_____

_____

_____

4. II Corinthians 5:16-19 is a classic passage which shows why we may become a bridge between heaven and earth. One way that we allow Scripture to speak to us more deeply is by putting its truths in our own words. Try paraphrasing the sentences or phrases in this passage that mean the most to you.

_____

_____

_____

_____

_____

_____

_____

_____

_____

_____

_____

Notes

Notes

Unlimited Possibilities

Imagine enrolling in a course on marriage enrichment. You purchase the materials and commit yourself to listening attentively during the ten sessions. But then you find that the lecturer actually says nothing about husbands and wives. Imagine purchasing a new cookbook which advertises 100 delicious dishes. But thumbing through it at home, you discover there are no measurements given for any ingredients. Imagine buying a do-it-yourself manual for home repairs—and then finding that the book says absolutely nothing about which tools to use.

That's what it would be like to tackle the challenge of soul-winning without the Holy Spirit. He is the essential ingredient that makes everything happen. The Holy Spirit is the One who gives power for witnessing. Successful outreach is always the work of the Holy Spirit, God's great power in the world.

Acts 1:8 makes the connection clear. Just before ascending into heaven Jesus told His disciples: **"But you will receive power when the Holy Spirit comes on you; and you will be my witnesses in Jerusalem, and in all Judea and Samaria, and to the ends of the earth."**

> *The greatest*
> *unused power in the world*
> *is the Holy Spirit.*

It was very evident that the disciples, in their own strength, would never be able to establish Christ's church on earth. The bastions of hell, the principalities of darkness, would definitely overpower them. But with the Holy Spirit's power these men, with all their weaknesses, could indeed become successful witnesses and spread the Gospel to the ends of the earth.

Let's look at some of the specific ways the Holy Spirit empowers us for service.

THE HOLY SPIRIT:

- Convicts
- Converts
- Imparts
- Commissions

The Holy Spirit brings conviction.

When any man or woman turns toward God, we can know that the Holy Spirit has been working to draw them to Him. The Spirit's work is fundamental, essential. He convicts people of sin and of their need of Jesus Christ. When some secular businessman without a shred of interest in religion suddenly begins to think about life's meaning, the Holy Spirit is working. When some youth addicted to drugs begins to feel that he's made a mess of his life and longs for something better, the Holy Spirit is working.

The Holy Spirit produces conversion.

The same Spirit who makes us aware of our need for change also enables us to change. He replaces the deeds of the flesh with the fruits of the Spirit—such as love, joy,

peace, and self-control. The Spirit is the active agent of transformation in our lives. As Paul put it: "I pray that...he may strengthen you with power through his Spirit in your inner being, so that Christ may dwell in your hearts through faith." (Ephesians 3:16, 17)

The Holy Spirit imparts gifts.

As I Corinthians 12 informs us, the Spirit gives to Christ's body various abilities for various kinds of ministry, just as our Creator gave the human body various organs to perform various functions. All these gifts combine to make the church's witness powerful and effective.

The Holy Spirit commissions.

He is the One who sends us out to proclaim the Good News. We see in the New Testament that the Holy Spirit always glorified Christ. He shares that same fundamental motivation with us.

During an evangelistic crusade in Sweden, I once challenged my staff to find at least one person they could lead to Christ during our three weeks of meetings. Afterward my translator told me that he felt quite uncomfortable when he heard this. He realized that he knew of no one he could see making such a commitment in that short time. But this man went upstairs to the chapel and began to pray, telling the Lord about his problem.

"Please, dear Lord," he said, "in the next three weeks lead me to a person through your Holy Spirit that I can lead to Jesus and the truth. I can't see this happening with my eyes, but I believe You'll do it."

An hour after he got up from his knees the telephone rang. This man answered the call and heard someone say, "You're not going to believe this, but for the last two years I've been studying the Voice of Prophecy Bible lessons and the Lord has impressed me that these things are true. I'd like to know how to become a Seventh-day Adventist."

The Holy Spirit is eager to commission us to help in His work. If we just take the first few steps, He will use us.

Let's look at five things we can know about the gifts of the Spirit:

SPIRITUAL GIFTS ARE:

- Given by God to Each Believer
- Of Equal Importance
- A Source of Unity
- Developed by Use
- The Foundation of a Witnessing Church

1. Spiritual gifts are given by God to each believer.

We know, first of all, that the Holy Spirit is available to all who believe in Christ. In one of Peter's first sermons after Pentecost, he told a crowd of people who'd come under conviction to repent and be baptized for the forgiveness of sin. And then he promised: "And you will receive the gift of the Holy Spirit. The promise is for you and your children and for all who are far off—for all whom the Lord our God will call." (Acts 2:38, 39)

This promise is for us today. Believers can claim the gift of the Holy Spirit—in all His fullness. And what's more, they can claim the gifts that the Holy Spirit imparts. In I Corinthians 12, Paul makes clear that the church, the body of Christ, has been given the gifts of the Spirit. And he concludes: "Now you are the body of Christ, and each one of you is a part of it." (v. 27) Each one of us has a part in the Spirit's gifts. Our special gifts will be in harmony with our natural talents and abilities; the same God who created us also gives us the Spirit. And these gifts will be useful in enlarging the kingdom of God.

> ## *"But the gifts of the Spirit are promised to every believer according to his need for the Lord's work."*
>
> Desire of Ages, p. 823

Each one of us needs to grasp this thought. We are individually gifted. We are part of Christ's body with a special role to play, special abilities to use.

2. Spiritual gifts are of equal importance.

Another point strongly emphasized in I Corinthians 12 is that all the gifts of the Spirit are of equal importance. There are no superior gifts or inferior gifts. As Paul said in his analogy, the eye can't say it's more important than the hand, or the head say it's more valuable than the feet. Every gift imparted is needed; it's essential. God doesn't bestow anything inferior.

We've all heard about the work of Billy Graham, the famous evangelist. But what about Ruth Goodge? For thirty years, this woman preceded Graham into cities targeted for a campaign and organized round-the-clock prayer groups, interceding with God on behalf of the people there. There's a plaque at the Billy Graham Evangelistic Museum in which the evangelist attributes his success largely to this woman and her ministry of prayer.

Billy Graham's preaching needed the power of prayer behind it. Ruth Goodge's earnest prayers needed a proclaimer of the Good News in front of them. The Spirit's gifts are all essential, all of equal importance.

3. Spiritual gifts are a source of unity.

These gifts bind the body of Christ, the church, together. Spiritual gifts enable us to recognize we are not all the same. Each one of us has been given different gifts by God. Where I may be weak, my fellow church member may be strong. I can appreciate others more for the gifts God has given them knowing that together we will accomplish the task.

4. Spiritual gifts are developed by use.

One thing to remember is that these gifts don't always appear full blown. God usually doesn't zap us with a fully mature spiritual gift, it must be developed by use. The more we experiment with and try out our abilities, the more complete and well-defined they become.

When I was studying theology in college, one of the things I dreaded most was student preaching. I was terrified of speaking in public! My hands would shake, my face turn red. I believed that I was called to proclaim the Good News, but my gift certainly wasn't well developed. Fortunately a friend suggested that I practice speaking in a room by myself. So I began my preaching in a closet of the school gym, delivering the Word to shelves of basketballs. And with practice, this ability did eventually mature; I was able to fulfill my calling and minister through preaching.

> *God usually doesn't zap us with a fully mature spiritual gift; it must be developed by use.*

The Spirit's gifts are to be developed. They don't just drop out of the sky on our heads; we need to nurture them to maturity.

5. Spiritual gifts are the foundation of a witnessing church.

Some people have the idea that spiritual gifts are primarily for ministry within the church. They certainly are useful for building up the body of Christ. But, we must remember that the Spirit is the One who empowers us for witnessing, the Spirit glorifies Christ. So the primary thrust of spiritual gifts must be to create outreach in the church.

> *Primarily, spiritual gifts create outreach in the church.*

If we have the gift of hospitality, let's use it to bring nonbelievers into our homes.

If we have the gift of encouragement, let's seek out those lost people in the world who are hurting and seek to bring comfort.

If we have the gift of teaching, let's find those people who are opening up to the Bible and teach them.

If our gift is giving, let's make sure that our funds result in meaningful outreach for the church.

Now, let's say you have accepted the fact that the Spirit has gifted you for service, but can't seem to get a handle on what your special gift is. How do we discover just what abilities the Spirit has given us? Here are five steps that will be helpful:

1. Ask God for wisdom.

The first thing you need to do is get down on your

knees and seek God's thoughts on the matter. James tells us very simply: "If any of you lacks wisdom, he should ask God. . . ." (1:5) Open up your life to the Lord and ask for His insight into how you can best serve as His ambassador.

2. Believe God has given you gifts.

Express your faith to God in prayer. Tell Him that you accept His Spirit and thank Him for bestowing spiritual gifts on you.

3. Dedicate your life to service.

The discovery of spiritual gifts is not some intellectual game we play; it's not just a matter of curiosity. The Spirit's gifts are for service. Tell the Lord that you are willing to use your abilities for Him. Consecrate your gift to His service ahead of time.

4. Explore various witnessing opportunities.

Begin with some form of outreach that appeals to you or for which you seem to have an aptitude. There's no substitute for action, participation. It's very difficult to just think our way into a gift. If you find that you are successful at a certain kind of ministry or that you find it very satisfying, you'll have a good indication that God has gifted you in that area. The important thing is to try something for Christ; use your abilities. Even if you're not very successful at first, keep experimenting. You'll soon see God do something through you; He'll begin opening your mind to many creative possibilities.

5. Seek counsel and confirmation from others.

Often other people can see things in us which we can't.

Notes

Other believers can also help us see where we've been successful and where we haven't. It's good to get feedback from those around us who have some familiarity with spiritual gifts. Their counsel will help ensure we arrive at a sound decision.

DISCOVERING YOUR GIFTS

- Ask God for Wisdom
- Believe God Has Given You Gifts
- Dedicate Your Life to Service
- Explore Varying Witnessing Opportunities
- Seek Counsel and Confirmation From Others

This world would be turned upside down, our communities would be transformed, if each one of us began exercising the gifts God has given us to win people to Christ. The Holy Spirit does not have to remain the earth's greatest unused power. **He can transform our church into an unstoppable force for the Gospel.** Let's each commit our gifts to Christ's service, for the advancement of His kingdom.

"But you will receive power when the Holy Spirit comes on you; and you will be my witnesses in Jerusalem, and in all Judea and Samaria, and to the ends of the earth."
Acts 1:8

DISCUSSION AND SHARING TIME

1. What is the role of the Holy Spirit in witnessing?

_____

_____

_____

_____

_____

2. What spiritual gifts do you believe God has given you?

_____

_____

_____

_____

_____

3. How have you attempted to use these gifts in witnessing?

_____

_____

_____

_____

_____

4. Talk about last week's assignment. Were you able to find out where your friend is on the line of spiritual interest? Did you make any unexpected discoveries about him or her? Were you able to nudge anyone up the line?

_____

_____

_____

_____

_____

ASSIGNMENT

Continue your efforts to meet felt needs in those you hope to reach, to identify their state of spiritual interest, and to develop that interest further.

INTERACTION WITH THE WORD

Notes

1. How did Paul express the potential of the Spirit, the greatest unused power in the world? (Ephesians 3:20)

_____

_____

_____

_____

_____

2. Note how Paul emphasized the importance of sharing the Gospel through the power of the Spirit. (I Thessalonians 1:5)

_____

_____

_____

_____

_____

3. In advising Timothy, how does Paul imply that a spiritual gift must be nurtured on a continual basis? (I Timothy 4:14)

_____

_____

_____

_____

_____

4. Spiritual gifts are listed in I Corinthians 12:7-11, Romans 12:3-9, and Ephesians 4:1-5. Try to write down a functional definition for the ones which appeal to you. You may get help from a commentary or Bible dictionary.

_____

_____

_____

_____

_____

_____

_____

_____

_____

_____

_____

An Exciting Way To Get Involved

Picture Moses about to enter the palace of the greatest monarch of his day and demand freedom for the people of Israel. Moses, at the time, was a meek herder of sheep, without any apparent eloquence or self-confidence. But still he walked into Pharoah's throne room, clinging only to his faith in God and a shepherd's staff. It was all he had, but it was enough. Because Jehovah had directed him to use that old stick to perform miracles, he used the thing he had in his hand. And Jehovah expressed His power through it, turning the waters of the mighty Nile into blood.

This is what God says to each of us, "Use what you have in your hand; use the gift you've been given."

When Jesus was confronted with 5,000 hungry families by the Lake of Galilee, He directed the disciples to use the thing in their hands. It was only five loaves and two fishes, but it was enough. "Bring it to me," the Master commanded. Jesus multiplied the 'insignificant' gift of a child into a feast for the multitudes. Always remember this: little in the hands of Jesus is much. Christ says to each one of us, "Bring your loaves and fishes to Me, bring your gifts to Me, and I will consecrate them for service and bless them and multiply them."

> *Use what you have
> in your hand.*

An oil company executive in London brought his gift to God. Although extremely busy, traveling all over England on business, he committed his life to soul-winning. This man had an interest in teaching, so he conducted Daniel and Revelation Seminars. Fourteen of my first baptisms in Europe came through this man's efforts; he'd dedicated his "shepherd's staff" to the Lord.

An older couple in the Midwest dedicated the thing in their hand to the Lord, too. Not especially gifted at preaching or teaching, they decided they could reach out with good homemade soup and homemade bread. So they targeted some young couples in their neighborhood and had them over for some delicious homemade food. As they talked afterward, the husband would share his conversion story. Soon their church sparked to life because these new couples began attending.

> ### *Little in the hands of Jesus is much.*

Gifts in small groups.

Now, let's talk about a way in which we can exercise our gift. The Bible not only reveals the gifts which God uses in His service, it also suggests a model for how they can be organized. Paul talks about the Spirit's gifts in the context of the body of Christ, and how a human body works.

If we study anatomy, we soon discover that the organs of the body are actually organized into different systems: the digestive system, for example, includes the stomach and intestines; the cardiovascular system includes the heart, veins, and arteries. We also have the skeletal system and respiratory system.

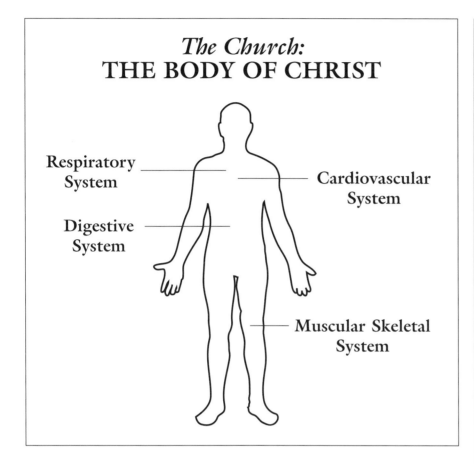

The Church:
THE BODY OF CHRIST

Respiratory System

Cardiovascular System

Digestive System

Muscular Skeletal System

Spiritual gifts are like the organs of the body with their specialized function. They work best when organized into systems or groups. Our bodies are not just a lump of separate organs free-lancing away at their functions. Each bodily function is organized into a tightly-knit system which works together toward a common goal.

All this tells us something about the environment in which we can best use our gifts. It's pretty hard to function alone; it's easy to get discouraged. But when we group with other people who have similar gifts and similar burdens, we find that our efforts can be much better focused and greatly magnified.

Small groups provide the best environment in which to exercise our gifts. They can become the action units of a local congregation.

Groups in Scripture.

Scripture itself gives us key examples which show the value of small groups in God's work. When Moses was overwhelmed by the task of leading the children of Israel, and dealing with all their problems, his father-in-law, Jethro, came up with a providential plan which saved the day, ". . . select capable men from all the people," he advised, "and appoint them as officials over thousands, hundreds, fifties, and tens." (Exodus 18:21) Every individual in the camp of Israel found himself in a group of ten, led by a godly official. Small group specialists tell us that the ideal size for group interaction is between six and twelve people.

Christ organized His ministry on the same principle. His master plan for evangelism actually centered around the teaching of 12 men; Jesus poured His life into 12 disciples. He didn't build His church primarily around the multitudes who followed Him, but around a small group. And those 12 disciples in turn were to make their own disciples, form their own small groups, and continue the process of multiplication.

Ellen White also gives valuable counsel regarding small group ministry:

> "If there is a **large number** in the church, **let the members be formed into small companies**, to work not only for the church members, but for unbelievers. If in one place there are only two or three who know the truth, let them form themselves into bands of workers. Let them keep their bond of union unbroken, pressing together in love and unity, encouraging one another to advance . . . As they work and pray in Christ's name, their numbers will increase. . . ."
> *Testimonies, Vol. 7, p. 22*

SMALL GROUPS	
A DIVINE PLAN	
The Old Testament Basis	Moses
The New Testament Basis	Jesus
Counsel to the Remnant	E.G. White

When people press together and begin exercising a common gift, encouraging each other—their numbers will increase. That's a wonderful promise. Even two or three people forming a group in this way can become a part of God's great multiplying ministry.

Every place in the world where the Adventist church is growing rapidly, that growth is the result of the activity of small groups organized for service. In the Philippines, where membership exploded from 75,000 in 1960 to 275,000 in 1988, I saw the church organized into Action Units for Service. Sabbath School classes often become the small groups, assigned to a certain territory, in which men and women can exercise their gifts toward a common goal.

In Seoul, Korea, Dr. Paul Yong Ye Cho's congregation has become the largest Protestant church in the world, with over 500,000 members. In 1964 this pastor had 3000 members and experienced physical and mental exhaustion from trying to minister to all his parishioners. But then he discovered in Exodus God's plan for small group ministry. He called his mother-in-law to his hospital bedside. They divided the church into small groups who could then do ministry in their particular areas of Seoul. The plan worked well, to say the least. As you can see from the chart on the next page, Pastor Cho's Full Gospel Church has expanded rapidly as the small group ministry has expanded.

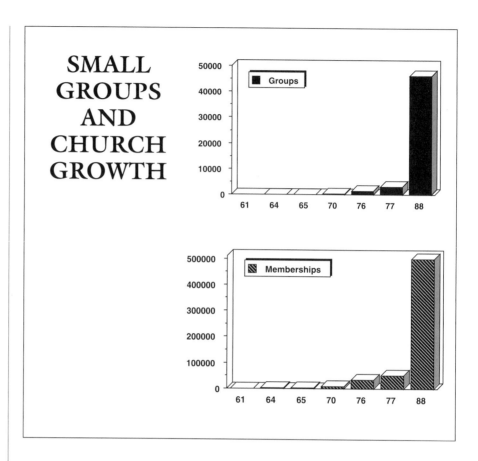

Small groups do indeed become a vehicle through which the Spirit enables our numbers to increase. How about forming or joining a small group in your church? Start thinking of people you could join together within a common bond of service. **It will help to have clearly in mind the purpose and objectives of your small group.** Here are some guidelines.

Commitment to a common task.

First, make sure you have a goal in common, a particular ministry which each member feels a desire to do. Make this the central bond for the group; you are together trying to accomplish a common task—perhaps personal visitation, hospitality ventures, passing out literature, starting health classes, or conducting Daniel or Revelation Seminars. When people move together in the same direction, closeness and mutual support naturally follow.

Intercessory prayer.

Begin praying for those people you intend to reach. **Specific prayer is always more effective than vague requests.** Claim promises for people by name. God wants us to pray for individuals just as much as He wants us to work for individuals. Both are efforts He can use.

Training for service.

Work together to develop your gifts. Group members can help each other a great deal in this area. You may also want to attend training sessions together or study training materials as a part of your group activity.

Shared witnessing activities.

Go out together and practice exercising your gift. There's no substitute for **doing**. There's a world of difference between telling someone they should witness and taking them out and showing them how to witness. Hopefully your group leader can be the one to take other members through the first steps. Just a few positive experiences will generally be enough to get most people well on their way.

Small groups work!

Fellowship.

Share your experiences with each other; give and get feedback. Rejoice together over successes and work together over the challenges. A small group is the best place where we can fulfill the Biblical command to encourage each other and build each other up. Share your common life in Christ together.

Notes

Small groups work! People uniting their gifts in service, people focusing the power of the Spirit for service, are a mighty weapon in the Lord's hands.

I remember sharing these principles in a small church in London which had been losing members for years. Nine lay people in that congregation caught the vision. They committed themselves to meet together and pray together. Soon they decided to make each of their homes an evangelistic center. The group members learned how to exercise their gifts in various ways and were able to bring 40 non-Adventist visitors to these homes for Revelation Seminars. This resulted in the baptism of 17 people, and that church, which had been slowly dying, came to life and became a growing congregation.

This is the body of Christ in action: men and women pressing together and encouraging each other in outreach. I pray that each one of us will become part of a small group where we can blend our gifts, prayers, and fellowship into a great movement for Jesus Christ.

> *"The harvest is plentiful but the workers are few. Ask the Lord of the harvest, therefore, to send out workers into his harvest field."*
>
> Matthew 9:37,38

DISCUSSION AND SHARING TIME

Notes

1. Why do you think Jesus instructed us to develop small groups as a basis for service? Have you ever been motivated to witness after a training seminar and then given up shortly after beginning? How can small groups help keep your motivation high?

_____

_____

_____

_____

2. What makes some small groups succeed while others fail? What are the characteristics of a dynamic, spiritually uplifting small group?

_____

_____

_____

_____

3. Have you ever had a positive experience, involving a small fellowship group? Share about that. How would you go about establishing a small group for outreach?

_____

_____

_____

_____

4. Talk about last week's assignment. How are things going? Share any successes you've had in meeting felt needs and cultivating spiritual interest.

ASSIGNMENT

This week try to find an opportunity to share some of your testimony with the person or persons you're reaching out to. As you attempt to cultivate spiritual interest, you'll find that sharing from your own life, things that apply to their need, is extremely effective.

INTERACTION WITH THE WORD

1. Note how Paul saw his ministry in terms of discipling a succession of groups. List the four generations mentioned in II Timothy 2:2.

_____

_____

_____

_____

2. What principles for small group interaction can you glean from Paul's beautiful picture of fellowship in Philippians 2:1-5?

_____

_____

_____

_____

3. Note how united in purpose the believers in Acts were, pooling all their resources for the task of proclaiming the good news. How far did their commitment extend? (Acts 4:32-35) In what ways could you express your commitment to each other as a group of believers?

_____

_____

_____

_____

Meet the Master

A man trapped in a cold, dark pit cried out for someone to help him. Buddha came walking by, the story says, peered down, and said to the man, "The reason you are in the pit is because you treated others unjustly in a past life. If you learn the lessons of the pit and follow the inner light, you will be delivered." Then Buddha walked on.

A little later, Mohammed came by. He said, "Young man, you must bow toward the temple three times a day, follow certain fast days, and commit yourself to making a pilgrimage to Mecca. If you do this, you will be delivered."

Then the Carpenter from Galilee came on the scene, bearing nail marks on His hands. He slid down into the darkness, and, after great pain and struggle, succeeded in lifting the doomed man out of that hole—giving up His life in the process.

> ### *Christianity presents God seeking after man.*

The Gospel of Jesus Christ makes Christianity unique among all the world's religions. The great faiths of mankind address the how and why of man seeking after God. But Christianity presents God seeking after Man.

That is the most important thing we can communicate in our witness for Him—what God has done to reconcile human beings to Himself. The heart of evangelism is Jesus Christ, God's solution to the sin problem.

Sharing your faith means sharing what Jesus has done for you. We're beggars telling other beggars where to get bread. There's great power in pointing to the solution, to the Savior. Jesus promised: "But I, when I am lifted up from the earth, will draw all men to myself." (John 12:32) Jesus is the drawing power; Jesus is the Winner of souls.

People are best interested in this Savior by hearing about how He has changed your life. **We lead people to Jesus, we fulfill our role as His ambassadors, by simply talking about what He means to us.**

But how do we get to that point with people? How do we get from everyday interaction at work or at social gatherings to an opportunity to tell our story, our testimony?

One helpful step-by-step technique is summarized by the word FORT.

Family
Occupation
Religious background
Testimony

Usually, when we first get acquainted with people, we ask questions about each other's families. So, **show an interest in their family;** people will often open right up. Then we move to their **job** (although men sometimes talk about occupation first). Ask about what they do, what they enjoy about their work, etc. Share something about your-

self. By this time you ought to have established enough rapport to ask about their **religious background:** "Do you attend a church in the area? Were you raised in a religious home?"

When the other person talks about his or her background, you have an opportunity to talk about yours. Lead into the subject gradually.

> *People are best interested in*
> *the Savior*
> *by hearing about how*
> *He has changed your life.*

Talk about your spiritual experience in general, ask the person a few questions about what they've appreciated or been discouraged about in their own faith, and then relate some experience that either led you to place your faith in Christ or clarify your commitment to Him.

Remember, you are trying to share Christ. **Your testimony is not about the doctrines of the Seventh-day Adventist Church; it's first and foremost about what Jesus means to you.**

If your friend is not a Christian, then obviously he or she first needs to place faith in Christ before learning about any other Biblical truths.

If your friend is a Christian, then it's important to first establish fellowship on the basis of your common life in Christ before going on to other doctrinal topics.

Try getting your testimony down to two or three minutes. Focus on one particular experience that best expresses what your faith means to you.

Hopefully your testimony will awaken an interest in this individual to know more about Christ or how to

begin a relationship with Him. If the person does seem responsive, try to nudge him or her forward by a question, such as:

Have you ever wondered why exactly Jesus had to die?

Has anyone ever explained it to you clearly?

Have you ever thought about making a commitment to Christ?

If you were to die tonight, would you have the assurance that you'd be in heaven one day?

A great many people would love to have such an assurance. This gives you an opportunity to go through a few Bible verses that explain just how a person is reconciled to God. Here's one example:

We were created to enjoy fellowship with God.

Genesis 1:27: "So God created man in his own image, in the image of God he created him; male and female he created them."

God gave us freedom of choice from the beginning so we could freely choose a relationship with Him and so that genuine love could exist between us.

Sin separates us from God.

Tragically, in the Garden of Eden, Adam and Eve bought into Satan's lies. They came to believe God wanted to somehow restrict their happiness and turned their back on Him. This rebellion resulted in a broken relationship. All of us share in that tragedy. Our sins result in a broken relationship as well.

"But your iniquities have separated you from your God; your sins have hidden his face from you, so that he will not hear." (Isaiah 59:2)

"For the wages of sin is death . . ." (Romans 6:23)

Since God is the source of all life, sin and separation from Him result in death, spiritual death now and physical death eventually.

Jesus restores the broken relationship.

God's love would not allow Him to have the people He created perish, separated from Him. But He could not condone man's cruelty either; His justice required that sin be punished. Faced with this cosmic crisis, Jesus volunteered to solve the divine dilemma. He would enter the stream of time as human flesh; He would live the life Adam should have lived and die the death Adam should have died. This is the mystery which awes the universe. God the Creator, holy and omnipotent, became a man, endured isolation, rejection and mockery, lived a perfect life in our place, and bore the penalty of sin for us on the cross. Christ was willing to face eternal separation from the Father, eternal loss, just so we could be redeemed. Amazing grace, how sweet the sound.

"But God demonstrates his own love for us in this: While we were still sinners, Christ died for us." (Romans 5:8)

"God made him [Jesus] who had no sin to be sin for us, so that in him we might become the righteousness of God." (II Corinthians 5:21)

Christ's sacrificial death results in pardon for us; we can be accepted by God IN God's Son, Jesus Christ. Sinners are welcomed into the arms of a holy, heavenly Father.

We receive this reconciliation by faith.

"For God so loved the world that he gave his one and only Son, that whoever believes in him shall not perish but have eternal life." (John 3:16)

I like that "whoever" part; that includes you and me; it's universal. A restored relationship with God, resulting in eternal life, is available to all who will accept it as a free gift made possible through Christ.

"For it is by grace you have been saved, through faith —and this not from yourselves, it is the gift of God. . ." (Ephesians 2:8)

All we must do is pray to God, confessing our need and placing our faith in Jesus as Savior and Lord. If we do the confessing, He will do the forgiving. And when God forgives, our guilt is completely gone.

"If we confess our sins, he is faithful and just and will forgive us our sins and purify us from all unrighteousness." (I John 1:9)

God wipes away the record of the past and gives us a new future as His chosen children. We are free to grow to be more like the One who is so gracious to us.

This is the story of the cross. It's always new and fresh because it's the story of our Savior. This is the wonderful offer which you can extend to any interested individual. If they are responsive, lead them through a prayer of faith. Congratulate them on the decision. Give them an assurance of acceptance with God.

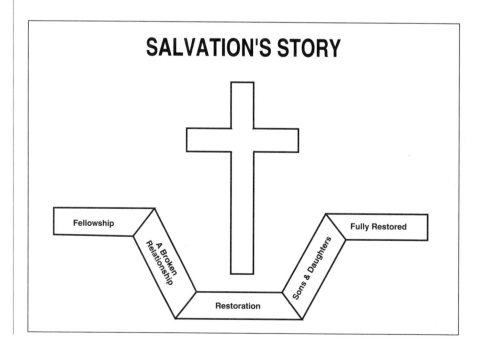

In the rather wild west of the 1800's, a young man from a good family background once lost his temper during a card game and shot a friend, who died. The youth was arrested, tried, and sentenced to be hanged. His parents, however, succeeded in getting sympathetic neighbors to sign a petition requesting the governor's pardon. Eventually, they were able to get thousands of signatures.

When this came across the governor's desk, he was intrigued that so many people would want to plead for a murderer, and so he decided to go visit the condemned youth in prison. He had a written pardon in his pocket, but he was dressed up as a clergyman in a black suit—to see how the boy would respond.

When the disguised governor walked in, the boy took one look and didn't want anything to do with him. He'd seen enough ministers. "I want nothing to do with your Bible and your Christ; I'm a dying man," he shouted.

It wasn't until later that this youth discovered, with inexpressible anguish, that he'd been visited by the governor—with a pardon in his pocket. His final word before the execution was this: "Tell the young men of America that I'm not being hanged because I murdered a man, but because I rejected the pardon."

We can tell the people we meet that they will not be lost merely because of their sins. Jesus has made provision for all our sins on the cross. They will be lost only if they do not accept the pardon that He so freely provides.

We have wonderful news to share. God has gone to such lengths to reconcile every human being on this planet to Himself. Our calling is to extend that invitation, and to show exactly how a person can be restored to a saving relationship with Christ.

DISCUSSION AND SHARING TIME

1. How do we get from everyday conversation to the point where we can share our testimony? (FORT)

_____

_____

_____

_____

_____

_____

2. What is our testimony about, first and foremost?

_____

_____

_____

_____

_____

_____

3. Share about the time and circumstances when the plan of salvation became most real to you, when God's saving grace struck you most forcefully.

_____

_____

_____

_____

_____

_____

4. Talk about last week's assignment. Were you able to share a part of your testimony to help an acquaintance? Were you able to relate your experience to his or her need?

INTERACTION WITH THE WORD

1. How did Paul express his determination to make Jesus Christ first and foremost in his evangelism? (I Corinthians 2:2)

_____

_____

_____

_____

_____

_____

2. Paul gave us a beautiful example of an urgent and eloquent appeal in II Corinthians 5:20-6:2. How does he communicate a sense of wonderful opportunity?

_____

_____

_____

_____

_____

3. Note how the writer of Hebrews forcefully emphasized how much has been revealed to us in order to keep us from "rejecting the pardon." (Hebrews 2:3, 4)

_____

_____

_____

_____

_____

_____

Notes

4. Write your own summary of the plan of salvation in four steps, using the texts in this chapter or others which you prefer.

_____
_____
_____
_____
_____
_____
_____
_____
_____
_____
_____
_____
_____
_____
_____
_____
_____
_____
_____
_____
_____
_____
_____
_____
_____
_____
_____
_____
_____
_____

Notes

A Step in Faith

Four lepers gorging themselves in an abandoned Syrian camp outside Samaria have something very pointed to say to us about soul-winning. They'd just wandered into the camp of their besiegers out of sheer desperation; everyone in the city of Samaria was starving to death. These men found that God had miraculously sent the Syrians into a panicky retreat and so they began feasting on all the provisions scattered about in the camp. But then they paused, looked over their incredible find, and said, "We're not doing right. This is a day of good news and we are keeping it to ourselves. . . . Let's go at once and report this to the royal palace." (II Kings 7:9)

Every believer has the privilege of feasting on an incredible find: the lavish grace of God manifested in Jesus Christ. Our fortunes have changed dramatically, in place of our own filthy garments, we suddenly discover that Christ's robe of righteousness is draped around our shoulders. We have the riches of the Word to nourish us continually.

We dare not keep such good news to ourselves. We must find a way to share it. This means taking a step of faith, setting a personal soul-winning goal. It's one thing to dream about reaching others for Christ. Many people can honestly say, "I'd like to win a soul," and never do anything about it. It remains a dream. But setting a goal is different; it involves a specific aim. Here's a good functional

---

*A goal is a vision
born of prayer.*

definition: **A goal is a vision born of prayer stating specifically what we believe God desires us to accomplish at this time, in this place.**

The great Biblical characters set goals. Abraham aimed at a city whose builder and maker is God. Moses set out resolutely to lead Israel to the promised land. Daniel never forgot the divine goal of setting Israel free from Babylonian bondage. Ezra and Nehemiah tackled the forbidding task of rebuilding Jerusalem and its temple from ruins by fixing on very specific goals.

Each of us needs a personal soul-winning goal. God can and will show you what that goal should be. Here are some principles which will help you.

Worthwhile goals are:

Spirit-inspired. Kneel before God and ask Him to give you a vision for your task. Ask Him to impress you with the gifts and abilities you have and how to best use them in your situation. The Holy Spirit will respond to your prayer. The best goals are not just whims or pet projects, but objectives that are clarified after time spent with God in prayer and in His Word.

Measurable. Worthwhile goals involve specific action, something observable, measurable. "I'll try to be a good witness this week," is an immeasurable goal. "I will dedicate three hours each week to Bible study ministry," is a measurable goal. We need a measurable activity so that we can tell whether we're achieving our goal or not, and so that we can begin a plan of specific witness. Of course our general witness continues all through the week. The way we act and relate to others on the job, at school, or at play, always witnesses either for or against the Lord. But generally, we need to aim at a specific witness in order to fulfill our calling as ambassadors of Christ.

Shared. As you are led by the Spirit into a measurable goal, it will help if you share that goal with other believers. Their counsel and encouragement can help you sharpen or modify your aim. Also, by sharing your goal you reinforce it. **"Expression deepens impression."** Talking about your objective will inspire others and deepen your own commitment.

Achievable. Worthwhile goals are realistic. A person with a family who works 40 hours a week may get inspired and commit himself to witness every night of the week. That's unrealistic. We have to take into account our other obligations. A commitment to spend one night a week, or one afternoon a week in specific witness is more reasonable for the typical individual with a variety of responsibilities.

Challenging. While our goal should be achievable, it also needs to stretch us a bit. The person who trains with weights always tries to lift a few more pounds than he has before. We need to stretch beyond casual or sporadic acts of witness. We need to take a step of faith and say, "With God's help, this is what I choose to accomplish each week."

WORTHWHILE GOALS ARE:

- Spirit-inspired
- Measurable
- Shared
- Achievable
- Challenging

Your personal soul-winning goal can be the vital step necessary to get you started in witnessing as a way of life. Goals are equally important to the church as a whole. One church growth scholar set about to study 100 churches in the Midwest and find out just what made small

churches small and big churches big. After a year, he discovered that churches which stay small tend to be very ingrown; they concentrate on their own problems. Bold faith goals through which a congregation resolves to reach out to the community were definitely lacking. Instead, church decisions typically revolved around fixing leaky pipes or selecting new carpeting.

It's said that the difference between the top five percent of society and the other 95 percent is simply a matter of goals. The most successful know where they're going, the others don't.

So, let's take a look at a cohesive master plan for growth which any church could use to become goal-oriented, to become outreach-oriented. There are five essential elements in a growing church.

1. Renewal

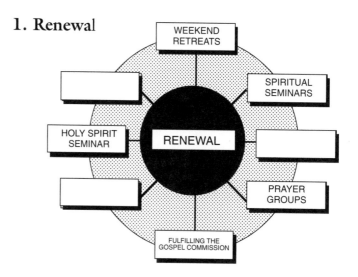

First, we need a plan for renewing the spiritual lives of the church members. How is revival nurtured in a congregation? Talk about it. Plan retreats, plan prayer groups, organize small group interaction. Plan the pulpit ministry and worship services with renewal as an objective. **Before God can do anything through us, the Holy Spirit must make something happen inside us.**

2. Equipping

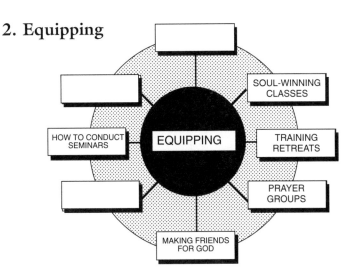

Churches do not grow unless they're equipped for service. As the Holy Spirit is given room to work and people are renewed, they need to be trained; **they need an outlet for their revived spirits.** Here's where soul-winning classes come in. We can teach people how to share their testimony, how to present the Gospel, and how to conduct health programs. The church needs to become a training center of Christian workers.

3. Outreach

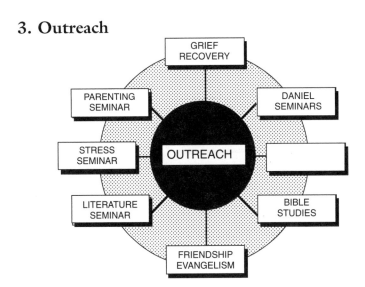

Now we can begin the different ministries of the church, giving members the opportunity to use their gifts in service. **Action is the essential climax of training.** Without it we just end up with more knowledge humming idly

in our head. Every revived, equipped believer should have a specific avenue of action, a way to act out his or her ambassadorship.

4. Reaping

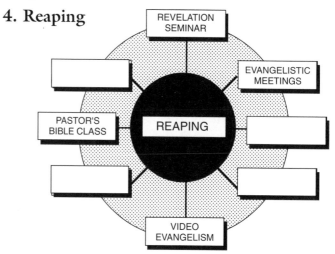

In this phase, all the people who have been interested and cultivated by various forms of ministry are given an opportunity to make a public commitment. This can happen through an evangelistic series conducted each year or through a pastor's Bible class. In the reaping process, we invite people to focus on and fulfill their ultimate need as human beings.

5. Nurture

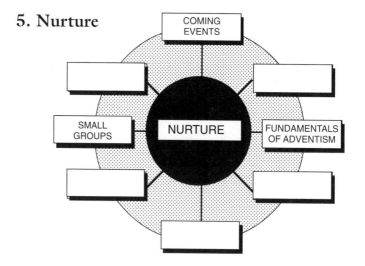

This is the follow-up stage of outreach. New believers need to be grounded in the faith. Now that they've made a commitment to Christ, they need to learn how to nourish that commitment each day — to develop a devotional life, to learn from the Word themselves, and to put it into practice. The church should have classes and small groups which carefully nurture babes in the faith.

With these five essentials of a growing church in mind, we're ready to put the whole process together and see the big picture.

> ## *Evangelism is a process, not an event.*

There is a **definite pattern** involving these elements. We begin with **renewal;** the Holy Spirit moves us out of our ruts. Then we are **equipped for service,** finding a way to express our faith. Next, we put our training into practice, **reaching out** in various ways to the community. This leads to a **reaping** of men and women for Jesus Christ and finally to their **nurture** in the faith. After all this, the cycle starts all over again. Growth continues.

Setting such goals as a church requires big faith, a big vision. But I don't believe for a minute in a little God. I don't believe for a minute that our church can't change the world around us. Let's get beyond our small plans and narrow thinking; we've got a wonderful message that every human being needs to hear.

Being a soul-winner, adopting a personal soul-winning goal, means being a risk-taker. We need to take some risks if we want to have an impact for God. Pioneers are willing to put their face to the wind; they're willing to swim upstream. Jesus Himself took the greatest risk by offering up His life for people who seemed only to ignore or mock His sacrifice. He risked everything for the joy of rescuing lost humanity.

Let's take our own step of faith with Him. Let's be bold, lay claim to a soul-winning goal, and see what God does through our lives.

GETTING IT ALL TOGETHER

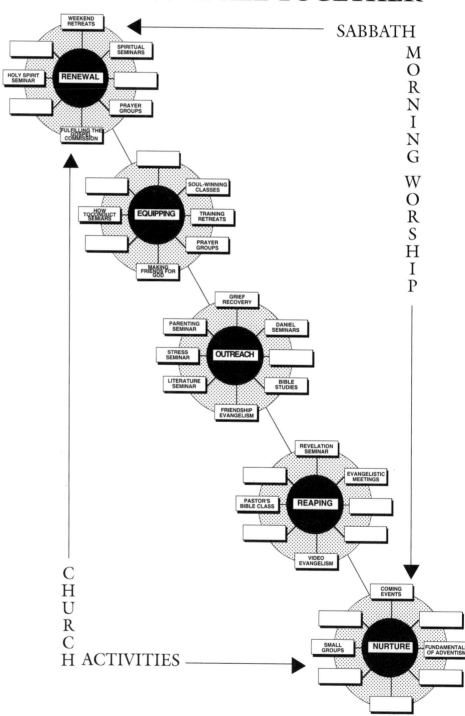

DISCUSSION AND SHARING TIME

1. Why is it important to set soul-winning goals?

_____

_____

_____

_____

2. Let's discuss the five characteristics of a worthwhile goal. Can you recall what they are? How can these characteristics apply to you?

_____

_____

_____

_____

3. What kind of personal soul-winning goal would you like to make?

_____

_____

_____

_____

4. Talk about last week's assignment. Were you able to share the plan of salvation with someone? How did they respond?

_____

_____

_____

_____

ASSIGNMENT

Adopt a soul-winning goal this week. Begin some form of outreach that you can engage in regularly. Perhaps you've developed friends who are interested who you could meet with regularly; perhaps you could begin studying the Bible. Or, maybe you could begin visiting people who have responded to one of our church broadcasts.

INTERACTION WITH THE WORD

1. Note the personal soul-winning goal Paul set for himself in Romans 15:20 and the conviction that led to it, expressed in Romans 10:13-15.

_____

_____

_____

_____

_____

_____

2. What assurance can we have as we attempt to formulate a goal that's right for us? (James 1:5)

_____

_____

_____

_____

_____

_____

3. In II Corinthians 9:6-11, Paul refers primarily to the giving which meets physical needs, but these verses can also apply to giving the Word. What encouragement do you find here related to adopting a challenging goal?

_____

_____

_____

_____

_____

_____

4. Try to respond to these passages by stating your own specific soul-winning goal — and the reasons for it.

_____

_____

_____

_____

_____

_____

Notes

The Demands of Love

The disciples trudged rather aimlessly along a dusty trail near the Lake of Galilee, their shoulders slumped, their heads hanging, all of them wondering how their bright hopes could have been so completely destroyed. Jesus had been crucified; He was gone. What could they possibly do now that would have any meaning?

Finally, Peter suggested a return to their old vocation: "Let's go fishing." They spent all night on the lake, casting their nets and coming up empty. In the morning, a stranger called out from shore, "Throw your net on the right side of the boat and you will find some." When they did so, the fish seemed to rush into their net as if drawn by a magnet. As they struggled toward shore with their unwieldy catch, John recognized the stranger as Jesus. In his excitement, Peter jumped out of the boat and sloshed his way toward the Master.

This disciple had denied his Lord three times; he'd forsaken Jesus at the hour of His greatest need. **Peter felt like a failure, like one who'd lost his chance forever to bear witness for the One who meant everything to him.**

But during the next few moments around a campfire which Jesus had made, this disciple would be reassured, restored, and recommissioned as an Apostle of Jesus Christ. The dialogue between Jesus and Peter illuminates the four demands of divine love and shows how that love restores to fellowship those who have fallen.

*Divine love
restores people.*

If you've ever felt like a failure, like you've let God down, if you've ever felt that you've ruined your chances to share Christ or feel that you've forever compromised your witness for Him, then Jesus' words to Peter are words for you. Divine love restores people; it recommissions us for service. Here's how:

Love demands a personal response.

After the disciples had finished eating the breakfast their Master had prepared for them, Jesus turned to Peter and asked, "Simon son of John do you truly love me. . .?" (John 21:15)

Jesus did not ask His disciple if he loved the cause or loved the message or loved the church. He asked, "Do you love me?" A personal relationship needed to be reaffirmed. The One who poured out His life in love for humanity desires to be loved; He desires to be loved by individuals.

> *There is a special place*
> *in God's heart*
> *for only you.*

Peter answered his Master: "Yes Lord, you know that I love you." I believe that Christ's heart beat a little faster when He heard that. I believe that expression of devotion thrilled the Master. Mrs. White writes in *Desire of Ages:* "Our Redeemer thirsts for recognition. He hungers for the sympathy and love of those whom He has purchased with His own blood." (p. 191)

If you have not responded to divine love, there is a vacancy in God's heart. There is a place in Him which only you can fulfill as His child. Every individual matters infinitely to our Lord. That is the basis of all soul-winning. That is why His love demands a personal response.

If a parent loses a child in some tragic accident, that mother or father is not consoled by the fact that other children remain alive. The head of a large family, for example, would never think, "Well, Bobby's gone, but that's OK; I still have eight kids left." No, Bobby's absence leaves an irreplaceable void.

There is a special place in God's heart for only you. No one else can replace the unique personality, the miraculous combination of genes and chromosomes, that is you.

And so Jesus asked Peter, "Do you love Me?" He longed for a personal response. He longed for an individual response. And He is still longing. We are motivated to reach out to individuals because of God's great love for individual human beings.

Love demands a genuine commitment.

After Peter had reassured Jesus about his love, Jesus told him: "Feed My lambs." Divine love is active, not passive; it's dynamic, not static, and so it seeks to draw an active response. The message is: "If you love Me, do something about it, express it."

> *Love compels us to act.*

Genuine love is more than a warm feeling, more than a nice idea; it involves commitment. Love compels us to act. Love is the husband getting up at three in the morning to change a wailing infant's diaper so his wife can get some sleep. Love is his going to work the next morning and not saying anything about it.

Love compels us to reach out to a lost and dying world, to a world of God's children in desperate need. We are compelled to share the news of what divine love accomplished on the cross.

When Jesus said, "Feed My lambs," it was both command and comfort. The Master called for a response to love. And He also assured Peter that he was worthy to minister again, worthy to feed the lambs. When divine love calls us to witness, it is both command and comfort.

Love demands continual growth.

Divine love always leads to growth. The more you love Christ, the more you are enabled and motivated to serve Him. And the more you serve Christ, the greater your love for Him grows.

In the dialogue between Jesus and Peter, we find two Greek words that are translated "love." Some scholars feel there is special significance in how these words are used.

Jesus' first question to Peter used the word "agape." He asked, "Do you **agape** Me?" That is, "Do you love Me with the same divine, unselfish love that I have for you?"

Peter replied, "Yes Lord, I **phileo** You." That is, "Yes I have a strong brotherly love, a human emotion for You."

Jesus asked the same question again, "Do you **agape** Me?"

And Peter answered again, "Yes Lord, I **phileo** You." It's as if he was saying, "I love you with all of the affection I humanly possess."

Jesus proceeded to ask the question a third time, but now employing the word phileo. "Simon son of John, do

WHAT IS LOVE?

- Phileo: Brotherly Love
- Eros: Earthly, Physical Love
- Agape: Divine, Unselfish, Heavenly Love

> ## *Jesus said:*
> ## *"Feed My sheep."*

you **phileo** Me?" That is, "Do you love Me with this human bond of affection?"

And Peter responded, the third time: "Yes Lord, you know that I **phileo** You." He was telling his Master, in effect, that he did give Him all his love, contaminated by human weakness as it was.

Then Jesus said, "Feed My sheep." Here we see Jesus' final recommissioning of His Apostle. I imagine Christ saying, through all this, "Then go ahead and work for Me. I know that you don't love Me with the same pure, divine love that I have for you; I know your love is human and comes through the channel of earthly selfishness, but I call you to feed My sheep. If you participate with Me in My mission, if you give your life to soul-winning, then you will grow into that pure, divine love."

Divine love asks us to start where we are. God helps us grow precisely because He accepts us right where we are. And then He nudges us down the pathway that will enable our love to mature and broaden.

However painful our failures may have been, however weak our love for Christ may seem right now, Christ asks us to get involved. God wants our love to expand. The more we serve, the more we will love. And the more we love, the more we will want to serve.

Love demands the ultimate sacrifice.

At the end of the conversation between Peter and Christ, we see the two of them walking together on the beach. As the waves swirl around their feet, Jesus tells Peter: "Feed My sheep. I tell you the truth, when you were younger you dressed yourself and went where you wanted; but when you are old you will stretch out your hands, and

> *Jesus wants us to give our life.*

someone else will dress you and lead you where you do not want to go." (John 21:17, 18)

In these words, Christ hinted at the martyrdom that His disciple would one day experience. His hands would be stretched out on a cross. In this revelation Christ offered Peter a choice. He offered him life's greatest joy, winning people for Christ. On the day of Pentecost he could see thousands come to faith. He could perform miracles in Jesus' name and glorify Him before many more thousands. Peter could have the joy of fellowship with Christ in His great mission.

But that privilege would demand a sacrifice, the ultimate sacrifice. Peter would be asked to give his life, not just his money, not just a part of his schedule, but his life. Jesus wanted Peter to make a commitment with his eyes open. And He wants the same for each one of us. More than giving of our time and our talents, Jesus wants us to give our life. **The divine love that holds nothing back longs for an ultimate commitment in return.**

One foggy morning in 1955, John Napoli, an Italian fisherman, guided his boat through San Francisco Bay. He was returning from a three-week sail and had nearly 3,000 pounds of fish on board. Then, suddenly, through the mist he saw a man floating in the water, desperately waving his arms. John steered his vessel beside him and pulled the man in. Then he saw another man and a woman and a child floating in life jackets. He kept fishing people out of the bay until over 40 were sitting, cold and wet, on the deck of his boat.

As it turned out, the hospital ship "Netherlands" had run aground in the fog and sent scores of passengers into

the waves. More and more survivors kept bobbing into view and John continued picking them up until there was no more room.

He decided to throw over a keg of fish and take more people on. But still there wasn't enough room. In the end, John Napoli dumped his entire 3,000-pound catch in the bay and crammed 50 survivors on the boat, with about 17 holding on to the gunnels as he sped toward port.

> *Divine love asks us to start where we are.*

For years afterward as John walked down to the harbor and his fishing boat, he'd meet people who would say, "That's John Napoli who threw the fish overboard and saved my life." Kids would tell their moms and dads, "Look, that's John Napoli who rescued all those people from the hospital ship." I don't think he ever regretted sacrificing his three weeks of hard labor at sea.

One day in a place where the streets are paved with gold, we're going to meet people who will come up and say, "Thank you for leaving your TV and coming to knock on my door to tell me about Jesus." "Thank you for putting off your golf game so you could give me a Bible study." **"Thank you for telling me about Jesus."**

Nothing we've ever done will seem like a sacrifice then. Our investment of time and effort, the investment of our lives, will seem over-abundantly rewarded.

Let's commit ourselves today to the things that really matter. Let's let go of some fish and become rescu-

Notes

ers. What a joy it is to turn love into action, to turn intentions into commitment. Let's respond to that divine love that holds nothing back by reaching out in service; let's fulfill our calling as ambassadors of Jesus Christ.

DISCUSSION AND SHARING TIME

1. As you have gone through this seminar, what specific commitments do you believe Jesus is leading you to make in your own life?

_____

_____

_____

_____

_____

_____

2. Are there readjustments in your priorities that God is calling you to make so you will have more time for outreach and soul-winning activities?

_____

_____

_____

_____

_____

_____

3. What is the greatest way to enhance spiritual growth?

_____

_____

_____

_____

_____

_____

4. Talk about last week's assignment. Were you able to begin fulfilling your soul-winning goal?

INTERACTION WITH THE WORD

1. What is John's alternative to love becoming a vague abstraction? (I John 3:18)

_____

_____

_____

_____

_____

_____

2. How does John define love's ultimate sacrifice? (I John 3:16)

_____

_____

_____

_____

_____

_____

3. What did Christ's love compel Paul to do? (II Corinthians 5:14, 15)

_____

_____

_____

_____

_____

4. Note how Paul ended his life of soul-winning on a note of triumph in II Timothy 4:6, 7 and how he was still faithfully feeding sheep while under house arrest up until his execution. (Acts 28:23-31) Write down the commitment you would like to make. What would you like to be doing until the end of time?

_____

_____

_____

_____

_____

_____

_____

_____

_____

_____

_____

_____

_____

_____

_____

_____

_____

_____

_____

_____

_____

_____

_____

Notes

My Personal Commitment

❏ I desire to recommit my life to Jesus Christ, allowing Him to use me in His service.

❏ As the Holy Spirit leads me, I will begin to pray for specific individuals by developing a prayer list.

❏ I am willing to commit _____ hours per week to service.

❏ I desire to be a part of a small group ministry trained in one of the following areas:

    ❏ Giving Bible Studies   ❏ Literature Ministry   ❏ Parenting Classes
    ❏ Conducting Daniel and Revelation Seminars   ❏ Divorce Recovery Classes
    ❏ Conducting Health Seminars   ❏ Children's Ministries
    ❏ Other _____

Name _____

Address _____

City, State, ZIP _____

Phone _____

My Personal Commitment

❏ I desire to recommit my life to Jesus Christ, allowing Him to use me in His service.

❏ As the Holy Spirit leads me, I will begin to pray for specific individuals by developing a prayer list.

❏ I am willing to commit _____ hours per week to service.

❏ I desire to be a part of a small group ministry trained in one of the following areas:

    ❏ Giving Bible Studies   ❏ Literature Ministry   ❏ Parenting Classes
    ❏ Conducting Daniel and Revelation Seminars   ❏ Divorce Recovery Classes
    ❏ Conducting Health Seminars   ❏ Children's Ministries
    ❏ Other _____

Name _____

Address _____

City, State, ZIP _____

Phone _____